999

Where's My Miracle?

Exploring Jewish Traditions for Dealing with Tragedy

MOREY SCHWARTZ

gefen גפן
publishing house בית הוצאה לאור
JERUSALEM ◆ NEW YORK   Est. 1981

Typesetting and Cover Design: S. Kim Glassman

ISBN 978-965-229-484-5

Edition   1   3   5   7   9   8   6   4   2

Gefen Publishing House Ltd.	Gefen Books
6 Hatzvi Street, Jerusalem 94386, Israel	600 Broadway, Lynbrook, NY 11563, USA
972-2-538-0247 • orders@gefenpublishing.com	1-800-477-5257 • orders@gefenpublishing.com

www.gefenpublishing.com

Printed in Israel   *Send for our free catalogue*

Harry Schwartz
1923–1979

Lillian Kaplan Schwartz
1927–1983

In memory of my parents,

whose suffering and untimely deaths

left me with many difficult questions…

Questions that sent me on a thirty-year quest for answers…

Answers that inspired me to write this book.

כִּי-אָבִי וְאִמִּי עֲזָבוּנִי; וַה׳ יַאַסְפֵנִי.
(תהילים כז:י)

Contents

ACKNOWLEDGMENTS

The author is indebted to those who served to inspire the writing of this book and to those who made its publication possible.

For encouraging me to think outside the box, and serving as a sounding board for many of my ideas, I am forever indebted to my father- and mother-in-law, Rabbi Ephraim I. and Esther Zimand.

I thank the staff, faculty, and students of the Florence Melton Adult Mini-School worldwide for providing me with an ongoing forum for open, text-based dialogue and discussion, enabling me to sharpen my teaching and writing skills, as well as heightening my level of tolerance for multiple views and opinions. Special thanks to Vivienne Burstein of the Melton Centre at the Hebrew University of Jerusalem for her kind encouragement and feedback on the manuscript.

I am grateful to Rabbi Moshe D. Tendler for being a role model for level-headed thinking during my years at Yeshiva University and RIETS and for confirming my feelings back in 2001 that the fatalist approach is not representative of the definitive Jewish approach to suffering.

Sincere thanks to Dr. Jay and Margie Robinow of Overland Park, Kansas, who provided me with support during a critical stage in my writing, enabling me to dedicate the necessary time to completing the research and beginning the writing process. They have also been instrumental in helping to underwrite the publishing of the book.

I offer many thanks to Ellen and Ronald Dimbert, also of Overland Park, Kansas, for their part in assisting with the book's publication.

I wish to thank Ilan Greenfield and the staff at Gefen Publishing House for their confidence, efficiency, and respect. They have made the publication of this, my first manuscript, a genuine pleasure.

I thank my children, Naftali, Yonatan, Leora, and Akiva for their ongoing interest in my writing, and for accommodating my monopoly over the family computer on many a Wednesday afternoon throughout the years.

And, to my dear wife Deena, thank you for being an invaluable voice of reason throughout our twenty-five years of marriage, for having such enormous confidence in my ability to reach this point, and for celebrating every milestone in this nine-year process.

PROLOGUE

WHERE'S MY MIRACLE?

Pounding away at the mattress I lay upon, the words "it's not fair" must have sprung from my lips a thousand times. With tears and a runny nose my badges of suffering, I wasn't going to get up from my position, face down upon the flowery deep-purple bedspread, until I was taught the answer to the eternal question of life and death. I was twenty years old, had just watched my mother suffer the debilitations of breast cancer, and had slept by her side in the hospital for many a night, just waiting for her to breathe her final breath. I had heard the doctor's words ring over and over in my ears, "she won't leave the hospital, she won't go home again."

It was late May in Schenectady, New York, where my mother had lived alone in our family home since I had graduated high school and pursued my college studies in Israel and New York City. I was an only child of parents who had divorced by the time I was eight. My father had died of cancer just four years earlier.

I recall the "by-the-book" trip, by ambulance, from that hospital to another nearby hospital, for a CAT scan, to check on the progression of the disease. The results would fall into one of two categories: very bad or worse. There was nothing to hope for.

We had been inside for many days. It wasn't a sunny day, but even under the cloud cover, the tall, leafy green trees of upstate New York, swaying in the wind, were stunning. The leaves rustled, as if chattering to one another, "there she is, there she is…" I thought to myself, this was my mother's very last chance to look at nature, to look at the beauty of the world around us. She kept her eyes closed, distraught at all of the moving around. "Mom," I whispered, "take a look out the window." I pointed out the large ambulance window to her left. She opened her eyes, looked in my eyes, managed to grin, and then closed her eyes again.

She didn't look out the window. She only looked at me.

Back to my teary-eyed demand. She is gone, only fifty-five years old. I am lying on her bed, still sensing her perfume on the pillow cover. "Why, why, why, it's not fair, it's not fair, it's not fair..." I say these words softly, I scream them at the top of my lungs, and I turn my head to the left, still resting on that pillow. I look out my mother's bedroom window; it's cloudy, anticipating a storm, with the wind blowing the green, climbing tree that reaches up to the heavens, way above our house.

And I wait for an answer. Surely there will be an answer, a voice out of a whirlwind... I am an observant Jew. I worked hard as a teenager to get to this place in life. I study the Torah and Jewish law daily. I pray three times a day. And I am only twenty years old! "God, it's just not fair!" I scream out. "Where's my miracle?!"

It would be years before I would discern my answer.

INTRODUCTION

DOES EVERY BULLET HAVE AN ADDRESS?

I entered the synagogue for services on Shabbat Parashat Nitzavim, September 15, 2001 (27 Elul 5751). It had been exactly one year to the day since Sgt. David Biri, 19, of Jerusalem, was fatally wounded in a bombing near Netzarim in the Gaza Strip. His death signaled the onset of the second Palestinian uprising, ultimately to be known as the Al-Aqsa Intifada. As of that Shabbat, 176 Israelis had been murdered in the name of a bloody uprising that showed no sign of relenting. (As horrific as it was, I could not at that time even begin to imagine that by Rosh Hashanah in 2005, the Intifada would take the lives of some 1,100 Israelis and leave nearly 7,000 others wounded.) And on that Shabbat, just prior to Rosh Hashanah of 5751, I was searching for meaning, for understanding, for comfort, and for hope.

We have no congregational rabbi in our synagogue here in Hashmonaim, a centrally located Israeli yishuv. For guidance and encouragement, we look to our favorite weekly Torah handouts, filled with words of Torah that relate to the weekly Torah portion, as well as providing Torah perspectives on current events. That Shabbat, the last of a year that had been filled with pain and despair, I reached for the words of Rabbi Shlomo Aviner of Beit El, a greatly respected Israeli rabbinic leader whom I considered to be largely in tune with contemporary issues as well as the needs of the modern Israeli people. Hoping to find inspiration, I turned directly to his article, entitled that week: "Does Every Bullet Have an Address?"[1]

An intriguing title, no doubt meant to grab the reader's attention. It worked. He had posed the inevitable question that had challenged us with the news of every tragic death and disfigurement during those painful

---

1. *B'ahavah u've'emunah,* publication of Machon Meir, Jerusalem, no. 321 (27 Elul, 5761): 9. Unless otherwise stated, all Judaic sources brought in this book are my own translations from the Hebrew, excepting quotations from Rabbi Joseph B. Soloveitchik, which are cited in the original English.

months: *Why did these 176 beloved brothers and sisters, parents, children, and spouses have to die? Why them, and not us?*

With great anticipation I began to read, in search of a thought, an insight that would help me to comprehend the senseless, random carnage of the past year. And there, in the very first word of the article, the rabbi's answer to this complicated philosophical issue was to be found: they all were meant to die, because "*every bullet has an address*"!

Citing a teaching of the Gaon of Vilna (Rabbi Eliyahu of Vilna, 1720–1797) taught by his student's student, Rabbi Yosef Zundel of Salant (1786–1865, Lithuania), this contemporary religious Zionist rabbi wrote, "It is a mistake, that which is commonly expressed in the world…that one who has freedom of choice can do what he wills to another human being without it being decreed by the Creator. Rather, in all things, it is decreed upon humankind even as to with which stone he will be pelted." If a person is hit by a stone, or downed by a bullet, it is a sign that so it was decreed from above. A person does not die unless it is so decreed by God. It is not possible that God can decree that a person live, and that the freedom of choice exercised by a murderer can trump that divine decree.

In fact, wrote this rabbi, if a person dies, it is not because of the rock or bullet, but rather because God decreed that his time had come. And so, he continued, should a soldier say, "I know that according to halachah I am obligated to join the fight in a *milchemet mitzvah* (a war fought for the sake of defending Jewish lives or for conquering the holy land), but I am scared," then say to him, "Do not be afraid, for *every bullet has its address*, there is personal providence." If his time has come, then the Angel of Death will find him wherever he is. If it is not his time, the Angel of Death will not be able to find him anywhere. If it is a mitzvah to endanger one's life in this war, then the soldier has nothing to worry about. And if a soldier goes off to war, in fulfillment of this mitzvah, and nonetheless something does happen to him, it is a sign that his end has come, his time is up. In fact, he would have died even if he had remained at home. It makes no difference to the Angel of Death. Wherever the man is, the Angel of Death will come to him; alternatively, the Angel of Death will make sure that the human being is in the precise place that he needs to be, at the precise time that he needs to be there, the place from which his life will be taken.

I was devastated. Was this the *Daat Torah*, the generally accepted philosophical stance that was meant to comfort and give meaning to the inexplicable tragedies that surrounded us? Was this the best explanation for the ceaseless slaughter of our fellow citizens? That it was their time!

I thought of Shalhevet Pass, age ten months, who, on March 26, 2001, was killed by sniper fire at the entrance to the Avraham Avinu neighborhood in Hebron. Shalhevet, seated in her stroller, was going with her parents to visit her grandparents. A Palestinian sniper opened fire from the Abu Sneneh neighborhood on the hill opposite. Shalhevet was fatally wounded by a shot to the head. Had her time come?

I thought of young Kobi Mandell and Yossi Ish-Ran, two fourteen-year-old friends who, on May 9, 2001, were found together stoned to death in a cave just outside of Tekoa, a community south of Jerusalem where they both lived. Was it really "their time"?

I thought of the twenty-one teenagers blown up on June 1 of that year at the Tel Aviv discotheque – had all of their times, coincidentally, all come at the very same moment? Were we to believe that each death, and the accompanying suffering, was meant to be?

And I thought of best friends Malka Roth, age 15, and Michal Raziel, age 16, and the Schijveschuurder family, parents Mordechai and Tzira and three children – Raaya, age 14; Avraham Yitzchak, age 4; and Chemda, age 2 – whose lives were snuffed out in an instant in the Sbarro Pizza bombing on August 9, just a month earlier. Strapped to the killer was a five- to ten-kilogram bomb, packed with nails, screws, and bolts, which completely gutted the crowded restaurant. Their three teenage sons, who had not joined them that day for pizza, were called upon to identify the mangled bodies. Was this too part of the divine plan?

I could go on and on...

I began to share this "bullet philosophy" with family and friends here in Israel, just to find out that most were in agreement with me – this explanation left much to be desired. It just was not satisfactory.

However, more than one responded, "Who are we to understand God's ways?" Uncomfortable as they were with the response of this well-known rabbi, they still felt compelled to accept his general premise, that all of this evil was somehow, for some reason, meant to be, even if it is not within our grasp to understand.

Of course, this is considered to be a foundational principle in Jewish theology, and it has formed the basis of the traditional response to tragedy for hundreds of years.

A man's steps are directed by the Lord, how then can anyone understand his own way?[2]

When faced with suffering, there are those who will search and find an acceptable explanation, finding some fault or some lesson to be derived from the tragedy.

Others will assume that there is a just explanation, only that it is beyond our ability to understand it.

However, even Ramban (Nachmanides, Rabbi Moses ben Nachman, 1194–1270), who strongly advocated for this second position, indicated that, nonetheless, such acceptance alone is not enough:

> It is the obligation of every being that serves God, out of love and reverence, to consider the circumstances and find a way to justify the [severe] ruling, to seek truth in the judgment according to one's limited ability…in order to acknowledge the judgment and the righteousness in that which seems to be beyond understanding….[3]

For the person who approaches tragedy in this way, this book will present many ideas, many possible "justifications" for suffering that have been cited by our great teachers throughout the generations. Perhaps this will assist such a person in fulfilling the challenge set forth here by Ramban – to not only accept tragedy as God's will, but to find justice and righteousness in it as well.

Then again, must there always be a reason? Is every tragedy meant to make a point?

As a former congregational rabbi, I have dealt with tragedy on numerous occasions, including personal devastation as a young man. I have discovered that these are not the only authentic Jewish theological responses to suffering offered by our sages. There are other approaches that, for one reason or another, have been forgotten or dismissed.

It was on that Shabbat, 27 Elul 5751, that I determined to write this book and to present and discuss those alternative traditions as recorded in our sacred texts. My goal in the writing of this book has never been for the

---

2. Proverbs 20:24.
3. Ramban, "Torat HaAdam," in *Kitvei HaRamban*, ed. Haim Chavel (Jerusalem: Mossad HaRav Kook, 1988), 2:282.

purpose of deciding which approach is "the correct" approach. There is no way of knowing. Rather, my intent is to expose the reader to the broad range of approaches expressed by our sages – classic Jewish responses that attempt to make sense of inexplicable personal tragedy. I present these classic texts woven together with present-day news items to help demonstrate their ongoing relevence to our lives.

I write this book with the understanding that different people will gravitate toward different approaches, finding personal comfort in very different ways. Experience has taught me that any single approach will bring comfort and meaning to some, and only serve to upset and anger others. I believe that I have found an approach within our rich tradition that best speaks to me, as will become evident to you, the reader.

My hope is that this book will serve to offer insight, meaning, and most of all comfort, in different ways for different people. I also hope that in some small way it will serve as a tribute to the memories of the victims of terror whose stories I have included throughout the book.

When it comes to issues of faith, it was Rambam (Maimonides, Rabbi Moses ben Maimon, 1135–1204) who pointed out that we are *not* obligated to believe one tradition over another. Addressing the reader, he writes:

> I have mentioned to you many times that in every disagreement between sages, where there are no practical ramifications, rather it is only a matter of belief, then there is no need to decide according to one of them [over the other].[4]

In his *Guide for the Perplexed*, Rambam indicates as well that this area of Jewish thought is open to personal opinion. Regarding the position of Judaism on the issue of personal providence, he writes:

> I shall let you know…what has been literally stated in the books of our prophets and is believed by the multitude of our scholars; I shall also inform you of what is believed by some of the latter-day scholars; *and I shall also let you know what I myself believe about this.*[5]

And it is with this significant imprimatur that I begin my work, and encourage you to find within these pages an approach that speaks to your

4. Rambam, *Commentary on the Mishnah*, Sanhedrin 10:3.
5. Rambam, *Guide for the Perplexed* III:17.

own personal sensibilities; a way of believing that makes sense to you. I will present multiple views on most issues, and will explain where my own personal thinking lies, at times offering a new reading of a traditional text in support of my thinking.

And so, it gives me great pleasure to invite you to join me on this journey of faith.

Chapter 1

FAITH AND FUNERALS

On a Tuesday afternoon, August 10, 2004, tragedy struck in Rehovot as two five-year-old boys burned to death when the storage shed in which they were playing went up in flames. The fire was so strong that the firefighters couldn't even tell that there were people inside. Only after seven minutes spent putting out the fire were the small bodies discovered. The Magen David Adom (Israel's Red Cross) worker said, "We have seen many things in the past, but this is much worse."[1]

One neighbor said that about 150 people gathered around, but were unable to do anything because of the intense heat from the flames. "Then we saw them in the corner, the two youngsters. There's no justice in the world. These two little children didn't do anything and they had to pay such a heavy price."[2]

On Tuesday, July 12, 2005, two sixteen-year-old girls, best friends since kindergarten, Rachel Ben-Abu and Nofar Horowitz, were on their way to the Hasharon Mall in Netanya when a Palestinian suicide bomber blew himself up and killed the two of them along with two others. Their funeral later that week lasted for about an hour, and was "punctuated by occasional wails of 'Why, God, why!'"[3]

What type of response is expected of a Jew when faced with injustice, inequity, or undue suffering?

Ours Is to Accept
When faced with suffering or untimely death, especially when it seems so undeserved, as in the death of a child or adolescent, we desperately search for meaning, for understanding. Unable to comprehend the seeming

---

1. *Jerusalem Post*, August 11, 2004.
2. Ibid.
3. Ibid., July 14, 2005.

injustice, some will attempt to comfort us by reminding us that it is not for us to understand, that the ways of God are not revealed to us. Instead, they tell us, ours is to accept, to know that there is a reason for everything that happens in this world.

The question I address here is what constitutes a legitimate Jewish first response to tragedy. Are we entitled to question the injustice, or are we expected to immediately affirm that what has transpired must be for the best? (In chapter 3 I will deal with the question of how we ultimately make peace with the inexplicable.) The following text and counter-text will demonstrate that there is more than one legitimate response to this question.

TEXT
Doubt Is the Root of Heresy

Said Rabbi Meir to his teacher Elisha ben Avuyah, "You have so much wisdom and yet you do not repent and return to your faith?" He answered, "I am not able." Rabbi Meir asked, "Why?" He answered, "For once I was passing before the Holy of Holies, riding upon my horse on a Yom HaKippurim that coincided with Shabbat, and I heard a *bat kol* [heavenly voice] emanating from the Holy of Holies, and it was saying, "Return, children, in repentance – except for Elisha ben Avuyah, who knew My power and rebelled against Me."

And that's all that happened, that's what brought this upon him?

Actually, once he was sitting and studying in the Valley of Ginosar and he saw a man ascend to the crown of a palm tree, reach into the nest, and snatch the mother bird that was roosting there upon her eggs. He descended the tree without incident. The next day, he saw another man ascend to the crown of the palm tree, take the eggs, and send away the mother bird. He descended, was bitten by a snake, and died.

Elisha ben Avuyah said: "It is written in the Torah, 'And you shall surely send away the mother bird and take the eggs, in order that it shall be good for you and you shall have a long life.' Where is the goodness for this man? Where is the long life he is promised?"

And some say that he saw the tongue of Rabbi Yehudah the Baker, who had been tortured and murdered by the Romans, in the mouth of a dog, dripping with blood, and he said: "This is Torah, and this is its reward?! This is the tongue that gave forth genuine words of Torah? This is the tongue that was engaged in the study of Torah all of its days? This is Torah, and this is its reward?! It appears to me that there is no reward and there is no ultimate resurrection of the dead."[4]

The legendary rabbi Elisha ben Avuyah is a tragic figure in Talmudic literature. At one time the sages of the first century CE were proud to recognize him as a colleague and Torah scholar of the highest regard; but later their opposition to him grew so intense that ultimately they even refrained from pronouncing his name, calling him instead Acher, "the Other." Apparently, something had caused him to lose his faith and to reject an observant lifestyle. A story is told of his blatant transgression of Yom Kippur that fell on Shabbat, riding on horseback before the Holy of Holies in the Temple in Jerusalem. He tells his closest student, Rabbi Meir, that as a result of this act of rebellion, he was forbidden from ever repenting. However, the Talmud itself offers an additional reason, one that seems to have trumped the one stated by Elisha ben Avuyah.

The Talmud tells us that the horse-riding incident alone is not what closed the doors of *teshuvah* (repentance) to Elisha ben Avuyah. Rather it was his reaction to a moment of seeming injustice that sealed his fate. When bearing witness to what seemed to be an incident that was not reconcilable with our trust in God and His equity, Elisha ben Avuyah openly expressed his feelings, verbalizing his critique of what he saw as divine injustice. This expression of doubt, this questioning of the divine plan, was considered to be the downfall of this great man, even more so than his public act of rebellion. For the latter he could still have been permitted the privilege of repentance, but for the former, his expression of doubt was considered to be beyond the pale, unconscionable and unforgivable.

The implication of this text is that only one who has no faith would dare to ask such a question, refusing to accept that there is always a just explanation of tragedy.

---

4. Jerusalem Talmud, Chagigah 2:1.

Elisha ben Avuyah's doubt became symptomatic of his impending apostasy, and so, expression of such doubt in the face of tragedy was considered to be an expression of heresy. As the Talmud explains, one must search and find divine justice in the midst of what seems unjust. Not to do so is to find yourself beyond the pale, outside of what Judaism considers a legitimate response to incidents that appear to be unfair and undeserved.

Ours Is to Question

The text we have just seen implies that questioning divine justice is symptomatic of one who has lost his faith, one who has chosen a path of heresy or apostasy. The counter-text offers a very different approach to verbalizing our misgivings.

COUNTER-TEXT
Even Moses Had Questions
Then said Moses, "Lord of the Universe, You have shown me his [Rabbi Akiva's] Torah, now show me his reward."

"Turn around," said He; and Moses turned around and saw them weighing out Rabbi Akiva's flesh at the market stalls.

"Lord of the Universe," cried Moses, "This is Torah, and this is its reward?!"

God replied, "Be silent, for such is My decision."[5]

In this story, Moses has just been time-warped into the future and introduced to the great Rabbi Akiva, who will be an important link in the chain of Torah tradition. Impressed with Akiva, he wishes to see what reward is in store for him, in recognition of his greatness.

God instructed Moses to turn around, an indication that what Moses was going to see was not what he expected. For daring to teach Torah publicly, Rabbi Akiva would be executed by the Roman authorities. The gruesome image he was shown indicated to Moses that Rabbi Akiva would suffer a horrible death, a demise that would lead to his mockery and defamation.

Moses was indignant. How could this be? This is not justice!

And then, without hesitation, the Talmudic storyteller boldly put the same challenging question into the mouth of Moses as we encountered in the story of Elisha ben Avuyah: "This is Torah, and this is its reward?!"

---

5. Babylonian Talmud, Menachot 29b.

Moses was rebuffed for his question, but the fact that the Talmud conveyed this story to us in this manner, with these same challenging words being spoken by Moses himself, implies that even Moses – who spoke with God face-to-face and had great faith in Him – could demand an explanation for suffering. Although his request for understanding goes unanswered, his questioning is not considered to cut him off from God. Placing these questioning words into Moses' mouth indicates that this is not only a natural reaction to inexplicable tragedy, but even more than that, it is to be considered a legitimate one.

Even if the answer is ultimately unfathomable, the question is not illegitimate. It is not the question of an *apikoros* (apostate) like Elisha ben Avuyah, but it is the question of the righteous Moses, and therefore is an absolutely valid Jewish question. If the great and most God-knowledgeable Moses is given the right to ask such a challenging question, we can surmise that we of lesser understanding are certainly permitted to question when confronted with injustice.

Of course, there is a tradition of biblical leaders not accepting unjust treatment of humankind. For instance, in the Book of Genesis, when God knew full well that He was going to destroy Sodom and Gomorrah, He decided to inform Abraham of these plans, giving him the opportunity to protest the destruction which was nonetheless inevitable. Abraham's objection and challenge of God's justice was neither criticized nor condemned by God. Even when Abraham uttered the words "It would be sacrilege for You to do such a thing, to kill the innocent along with the guilty, letting the just and the wicked fare alike! It would be sacrilege to ascribe this to You! Shall not the Judge of all the earth do justly?"[6] (a challenge to God echoed in the words that the sages placed in the mouths of both Moses and Elisha ben Avuyah), Abraham was not maligned for his misgivings. God did not lecture him, or tell him to be still and to accept the impending destruction as something that God was forced to do for the sake of some greater good.

The prophet Jeremiah, having lived through the destruction of the first Temple in Jerusalem during the sixth century BCE, expressed his great frustration at what he saw about him. "Right will You be, Lord, if I begin to argue with You, and yet, I will lay these complaints before You. Why do the wicked prosper in their ways? Why are the lives of those who betray

---

6. Genesis 18:25.

You so tranquil?"[7] Jeremiah was not punished for his desperate inquiry, nor did God provide a clear answer to his plea.

It would seem clear that the biblical tradition provides room to ask the question, and treats such questioning with respect. According to tradition, the Creator understands the thoughts of human beings, and is neither offended nor angered with such inquiries. The act of questioning can prove to be cathartic even when no clear answers are forthcoming.

Job Is to Be Commended

Along these same lines, most people miss the main point of God's reaction to Job's refusal to accept his undeserved suffering.

Job wrestled throughout the book to find understanding in his suffering. His three companions, rather than questioning or expressing dismay at his plight, attempted to offer Job rational explanations, related to understanding all of God's ways as ways of justice, and therefore conveyed to Job that he must have deserved all of his misfortune.

When God appeared to Job at the end of the book, it was not out of anger, but in a grand display of His power, "out of the whirlwind" (more on this in chapter 8). Job responded by admitting, "Therefore have I uttered that which I understood not, things too wonderful for me, which I knew not!"[8]

We think that's the end of the story. But the punch line is yet to come! It was after God had spoken these words to Job that the main point of the story is revealed to us. It is somewhat of a surprise ending.

> God turns to Job's close friend, Elifaz the Yemenite, saying, "I am angry with you and your two friends [Job's comforters] because you have not spoken of Me what is right: My servant Job did."[9]

What a major turn of events. Unbelievable! The whole story seems to have been leading up to the conclusion that Job was wrong in his refusal to find meaning in his suffering, and that in the end he would accept he was wrong. But instead, in the end the significant twist is that Job was right and his comforters were wrong! The conventional approach of theodicy, that Job must have done something to deserve his fate, is torn up and thrown out by God Himself. This is quite a powerful message, and serves as yet another legitimization of the tradition of questioning.

---

7. Jeremiah 12:1.
8. Job 42:3.
9. Job 42:7.

Everything God Does, He Does for the Best

Though confronted with our limited understanding of God's ways, we now however understand that the tradition provides us with at least two different ways to respond to apparent injustice. According to some, we are to assume that what seems unjust is truly just, only that we are unable to comprehend the bigger picture. And even more than that, the act of expressing our doubts or demanding explanation is itself a condemnable act.

According to a different tradition, we are not really expected to react with such confidence when we come face-to-face with suffering or inequity. It is, rather, to be considered perfectly legitimate to protest and yearn for understanding.

The concurrent recording in the Talmud of two incidents involving the great Rabbi Akiva seems to reveal ambivalence about the tradition.

TEXT
Rabbi Akiva's Admirable Approach to Hardship
So it was taught in the name of Rabbi Akiva: A man should always accustom himself to say, "Whatever the All-Merciful does is for the good," [as exemplified in] the following incident. Rabbi Akiva was once going along the road and he came to a certain town and looked for lodgings but was everywhere refused. He said, "Whatever the All-Merciful does is for the good," and he went and spent the night in the open field. He had with him a rooster, a donkey, and a lamp. A gust of wind came and blew out the lamp, a weasel came and ate the rooster, a lion came and ate the donkey. He said, "Whatever the All-Merciful does is for the good." The same night a band of robbers came and carried off the inhabitants of the town. He said to them, "Did I not say to you, 'Whatever the All-Merciful does is all for the good'?"[10]

Rabbi Akiva here related to his students a real-life experience, wherein he was exposed to some very serious inhospitable behavior. As he retold the story, he insisted that each step of the way he chose to accept his lot, reasoning that this was the will of God, and whatever God does, he does

---

10. Babylonian Talmud, Berachot 60b.

for the best. When the inhospitable town is ransacked and its inhabitants all kidnapped during the very night in which he sought lodging there, he was able to interpret all of his seeming misfortunes as blessings in disguise. For if the lamp had stayed lit, or the rooster or donkey remained alive that night, they may very well have revealed his location in the woods to the marauding bandits, and led to his demise as well. Almost like the biblical Sodom and Gomorrah, this town seems to have been destined to be attacked, and all that God could do was to prevent Rabbi Akiva from being swept up in the violence that was to ensue.

Like the person who misses his flight on a plane bound to crash, or the driver who makes a wrong turn only to avoid a violent terrorist bombing, Rabbi Akiva interpreted all that had happened to him as acts of God, and that all actions taken by God must, by definition, be for the greater good.

Everything Is from God

"This Is the Thing That Comforts Us"

On June 24, 2006, 18-year-old Eliyahu Asheri was kidnapped by Palestinian terrorists. Several days later, his body was discovered; he had been murdered shortly after his abduction.

Asheri's mother, Miriam, spoke on the day of her son's funeral saying, "What strengthens you is, first of all, knowing that everything is from God, knowing that to die sanctifying God's name, as he did – that God chose him to sanctify the name of heaven in public. This is the thing that comforts us. Any other comfort is trivial in my estimation; it doesn't let my spirit rest."[11]

One folio later, the Talmud returns to the events surrounding Rabbi Akiva's execution, the aftermath of which was witnessed by Moses.

COUNTER-TEXT
The Angels Question God's Justice
And while they combed his flesh with iron combs, he was accepting upon himself the kingship of heaven. His disciples said to him: "Our teacher, even to this point?" He said to them:

---

11. Based on the article "Thousands Attend Asheri's Funeral," *Jerusalem Post*, June 29, 2006; http://www.jpost.com/servlet/Satellite?apage=2&cid=1150885880814&pagena me=JPost%2FJPArticle%2FShowFull.

"**All my days I have been troubled by this verse, 'with all your soul,' [which I interpret as] 'even if He takes your soul.' I would say, 'When shall I have the opportunity of fulfilling this?' Now that I have the opportunity shall I not fulfill it?"**

The ministering angels said before the Holy One, blessed be He: "This is Torah and this is its reward?! [He should have been] among those who die by Your hand, O Lord."

He replied to them: "Their portion is in life."

A *bat kol* [heavenly voice] went forth and proclaimed: "Happy are you, Rabbi Akiva, that you are destined for life in the world to come."[12]

This epilogue to a story describing the torturous death of Rabbi Akiva provides us with much food for thought. It is somewhat ironic. As Rabbi Akiva was executed, he accepted his death as an opportunity to serve God with his entire soul, in fulfillment of the biblical command to serve God with all of one's soul. He accepted his lot as an opportunity, perhaps in the same light as he was pictured before, as one who would always say that all that God does is for the best.

Noteworthy, however, is the response of the ministering angels[13] to Rabbi Akiva's painful end. Here again, as in the cases of both Elisha ben Avuyah and Moses, the rabbis put the same piercing words into the mouths of the angels: "This is Torah, and this is its reward?!" We can't help but pause and ponder this scene for a moment. These are God's ministering angels, and even they are challenging the ways of the Almighty. "Akiva deserved better! He should have been taken in peace, by Your hand, not by the hands of these infidels!"

God informed them that there will be justice, for Akiva had gained access to the world to come; and sure enough, this claim was immediately confirmed to be accurate through the proclamation of a heavenly voice.

Appearing in the Talmud so soon after the previous case where Akiva asserted steadfast faith in the divine purpose of all that happens, this story seems to offer an alternative perspective by which to interpret the vicissitudes of life. While Akiva took an admirable approach, the

---

12. Babylonian Talmud, Berachot 61b.
13. According to most opinions, angels do not function autonomously but are strictly extensions of God. Their inclusion in texts such as this represents a literary device used to convey a teaching about God or humankind.

ministering angels took a very different approach. The fact that God did not silence them, but only comforted them, promising them that Akiva would be rewarded for his dedication to Torah, leaves unresolved their claim as to the injustice of his suffering. And even though Akiva chose to interpret his suffering as an opportunity to serve God with the sum total of his being, we do not get the impression that Akiva necessarily interpreted his execution as devised by God for the purpose of serving the greater good. Rabbi Akiva here testified to his personal faith in God despite the suffering he was forced to endure, and no one claimed, especially the ministering angels, that this was somehow "for the best."

Thus we have two traditions, one that praises the tradition of seeing everything that happens as emanating from God and always for the best, and a second tradition that questions the justice of suffering and finds comfort only in knowing that despite the suffering (not because of it) justice will be done.

This idea of divine justice leads us to our final text in this chapter.

Blessing on the Good, Blessing on the Bad

What we have said up until now is all well and good in philosophical terms. These biblical and midrashic accounts share different traditions as to what can be considered appropriate responses to suffering. However, a look at the normative way of Jewish living, a glimpse into the halachah (Jewish law), gives us some very specific directives as to how we are to respond to the good and the bad that we experience in our lives.

> For rain and for good tidings one says, "Blessed be He that is good and bestows good [*Baruch HaTov v'HaMeitiv*]." For bad tidings one says, "Blessed be the true judge [*Baruch Dayan HaEmet*]."[14]

The sages teach us clearly that both good news and bad news warrant the recitation of a blessing.

It is fairly clear that good news should be accompanied by a blessing. After all, it is common practice in Judaism to give thanks to God for the many blessings in our lives. In the times of the Temple, a special thanksgiving offering might be called for under such circumstances. In

---

14. Mishnah Berachot 9:2.

lieu of the Temple, at the very least a blessing acknowledging this good fortune is to be recited.

But what is the function of making a blessing when confronted with bad tidings?

Many are familiar with this practice as it is performed in the context of hearing news of a death. The appropriate response to news of a death is to say the words *Baruch Dayan HaEmet* (Blessed be the true judge). It is common practice today for mourners to recite this blessing at a funeral at the moment of *keriah*, the ritual tearing of a garment that provides an outward physical means of expressing one's distraught inner emotions.

It is commonly understood that this blessing is meant to express one's confidence that "whatever God does is for the best." He alone is the true judge who does only justice. It is commonly understood that the Mishnah cited above teaches that we are required to verbally affirm divine justice at the very moment we encounter distressful or painful news. As Rambam explains in his commentary on this Mishnah, "Many things are thought to be bad at first, and in the end they bring great good.... Therefore it isn't appropriate for one who is wise to become distressed in the face of immense sorrow...for he does not know its ultimate purpose." In other words, the blessing of God as "the true judge" serves to express our belief that what has happened must ultimately be for the best according to God's "big plan" for our lives. Like Rabbi Akiva, we affirm through this blessing that even though at the moment it seems to us to be unjust or undeserved, it is actually a consequence of God's true judgment and therefore it can only be for the good.

However, I am convinced that this is not the only way to understand the meaning of this blessing.

Did the sages actually decide to require us, at the height of our suffering – at the scene of a bloody terrorist attack, at the death bed of a dying child – to bless God, with great confidence that this is "all for the best"? For even if that is the case, as in the story of Rabbi Akiva's night in the woods, it is unrealistic to expect such an immediate response from most people amid the confusion of the moment.

In other words, it seems to me that in many instances the heart and the mouth of the one making this blessing will not be in the same place. The mouth might be saying, "This is all for the best," while the heart is yearning to understand the fairness and justice of what has transpired.

Therefore, I would suggest an alternative understanding.

The word *dayan* in reference to God hardly appears in the Bible. However, when it does appear, its context gives us a very different understanding of God as *dayan*, as judge.

> For the Leader. A Psalm of David, a Song.
>
> Let God arise, let His enemies be scattered;
> and let them that hate Him flee before Him.
>
> As smoke is driven away, so drive them away;
> as wax melts before the fire, so let the wicked
> perish at the presence of God.
>
> But let the righteous be glad, let them rejoice before God;
> yes, let them rejoice with gladness.
>
> Sing unto God, sing praises to His name;
> extol He Who rides upon the skies, Whose name is the Lord;
> and rejoice before Him.
>
> A father of the fatherless, and a *dayan almanot* [judge of widows],
> is God in His holy habitation.[15]

The context of this psalm is a prophetic vision for the aftermath of Israel's suffering at the hands of her enemies. God the warrior will drive them away from Israel, and the nation will once again rejoice. Here the term *dayan* is used in a way that makes it clear that we are not speaking about a God Who has righteously turned these women into widows, for reasons that are beyond comprehension. Rather, the psalmist assures us that God, as the *Dayan Emet*, will bring to justice those who have turned children into orphans and wives into widows.[16] This is the greatness of God, Who can make good on unjust, unfair, and seemingly insufferable events in our lives.

Therefore, in times of suffering, as in times of joy, our rabbis instructed us to make a blessing: *Baruch Dayan HaEmet*, Blessed is God, the Judge of Truth, for only He can, in this world or the next, judge the circumstances and balance the suffering.

In other words, we are not instructed in our darkest hours to express

---

15. Psalms 68:1–6.
16. See *Tefilot David*, Malbim's commentary to Psalms 68:6.

our confidence that this suffering has meaning or purpose. Our nerves and emotions are too fragile to demand such a response under such conditions. Rather, we are encouraged to have faith that there is fairness and justice, and that when suffering or pain is our lot, it is God alone – the Judge of Truth – Who can come along and right the injustice.

And so, when the ministering angels complain to God of the injustice they witnessed, as the skin of the great Rabbi Akiva was flayed with combs of steel, God does not silence them. He does not imply that they cannot understand the ways of God. Instead, He tells them to take comfort in the fact that God does not fail to compensate those who suffer in this world, and that Rabbi Akiva was already on his way to the world to come, where he will reap the great rewards awaiting him there.

God does not justify Rabbi Akiva's suffering. He reminds us that He is the *Dayan HaEmet*, the Judge of Truth, who has not abandoned Akiva, and that, in compensation for this undeserved suffering, Akiva would now enter directly into Paradise.

Is it appropriate religious behavior for a Jew to express words of doubt when faced with injustice, inequity, or undue suffering? As I have demonstrated, different texts and different understandings of these texts reflect differing traditions, offering more than one appropriate Jewish response to such dire circumstances.

Now that we have addressed the primary response to suffering, we will embark on a quest to identify the multiple Jewish understandings as to why human beings suffer.

Chapter 2

WHAT DID I DO TO DESERVE THIS?

Tradition of Reward and Punishment

> "If I have sinned, what have I done to You,
> O guardian of humankind?
> Why make me your target...?"
>
> (Job 7:20)

When faced with suffering – our own or that of others – then just like the ministering angels, we are naturally inclined to expect justice, and just like Job, we can't help but search for an explanation.

On May 25, 2001, in what was termed the worst building disaster in Israel's history, more than three hundred people were injured and twenty-three were killed when the dance floor at the Versailles Banquet Hall in Jerusalem collapsed during a wedding. Assi and Keren Sror had just become husband and wife, and many of their six hundred guests had streamed onto the dance floor for the heart-thumping dancing common at Jewish weddings. Joyous guests danced on one another's shoulders, kissing the bride and groom after the groom smashed a glass under his foot, marking the end of the ceremony and the beginning of the party.

Suddenly, the dancers disappeared as the floor buckled underneath them, plunging three stories. Screaming guests scrambled for safety; a handful peered into the crater in disbelief. Stunned celebrants grasped their heads in shock.

As is common in Jewish weddings, entire clans were invited to the wedding, a fact that only added to the tragedy as survivors buried multiple members of the same family.

The wedding had originally been planned to take place at a kibbutz on the outskirts of Jerusalem, near the West Bank. Israel TV said they decided to hold it at the banquet hall instead, because they feared the recent violence in the Palestinian territories.

A week later, a journalist covering the national reaction to the tragedy wrote about the affect the disaster had had on the Israeli people. With the Palestinian Intifada seemingly without end, the tragedy "convinced many Israelis that they are living in a hell on earth, suffering divine punishment for sins accumulated in decades of neglect."[1]

This response to tragedy, suffering, and death has a strong foundation in the words of the biblical prophets. One clear example is found in the words of the prophet Ezekiel, who teaches:

> Behold, all souls are Mine…the soul that sins, it shall die.
>
> But if a man is just, and does that which is lawful and right…and has observed My ordinances, been truthful, and just, he shall surely live, says the Lord, God.
>
> He that has committed…abominations, he shall surely be put to death, his blood shall be upon him.[2]

For some people, searching for meaning amid tragedy can be an important part of dealing with the event. It serves to provide an anchor for the person or the nation feeling tossed about in the storm. A rationale for suffering can be a source of comfort for one whose consolation comes from knowing that even when life has been turned upside down, there remains a semblance of order to all things in the universe. Just as reward is well deserved by those who have earned it, so too troubles are the fate of those who have erred, sinned, or otherwise missed the mark.

This worldview is very much a part of Jewish tradition. Our sages have debated the purpose of suffering for thousands of years.

Looking for Meaning in Death

The history of the Jewish people overflows with stories of martyrdom. We are exposed to these stories in an effort to inspire us with the sacrifices

---

1. Chemi Shalev, "Disaster Bares a Nation's Flaws," *Forward*, June 1, 2001.
2. Ezekiel 18:4–13.

made throughout the centuries to preserve Judaism and Jewish living. We are to see ourselves as a link in that eternal chain of men and women who have willingly given their lives for this sacred purpose.

Our High Holiday liturgy serves as an annual reminder of this type of sacrifice. We include therein the story of the ten martyrs, ten great rabbinic figures whose lives were mercilessly taken by the Roman conquerors of Jerusalem during the second century CE. The association of their selfless sacrifices with the observance of Yom Kippur, the Day of Atonement, is somewhat problematic. Reading of their deaths as part of the mournful liturgy of the Ninth of Av, as is our practice, is logical. It relates to the destruction and suffering we endured in the wake of the Roman conquest of the land. But what is its significance at the center of the Day of Atonement services? A look at this next text may provide new understanding.

TEXT
In Search of a Meaningful Death

Rabbi Yishmael ben Elisha the High Priest and Rabban Shimon ben Gamliel were on their way out to be killed by the Romans, when Rabban Shimon said to Rabbi Yishmael, "Rabbi, my heart goes out, for I do not know why I am being killed."

Rabbi Yishmael said to Rabban Shimon, "Has it ever happened that a person came to you for judgment or for a question and you delayed him until you swallowed what was in your bag or until you tied your sandal or until you wrapped yourself in your shawl? Remember, the Torah said, 'You shall not ill-treat any widow or orphan. If you do mistreat them in any way, and they cry out to Me, I will surely hear their cry.'"

And for this explanation, Rabban Shimon said to him, "You have comforted me, Rabbi."[3]

Rabban Shimon was actually among the first of the rabbinic leaders to be killed by the Romans, during the time of their siege on Jerusalem in 70 CE. Rabbi Yishmael was also killed and tortured by the Romans, but sixty-five years later. Most likely, this dialogue between the two of them never actually happened. However, the point the midrash intends to make seems quite clear. Rabban Shimon was the political leader, the *nasi* of the Sanhedrin at

---

3. Mechilta on Nezikin, 95b, paragraph 18.

the time of the destruction of the Temple. No other rationale needed to be established for his execution by the Roman authorities at the time. However, Rabban Shimon could not regard himself as merely a political victim of the Romans. His death had to be more than that, or else God would not have allowed it to transpire, especially in this demeaning fashion.

This aggadah (rabbinic tale) conveys the message that every death has meaning on a personal level, and every death is justified. We can rest assured that there is order and purpose, even in times of great chaos and turmoil.

TEXT
It Is Sin that Kills!

Our rabbis taught: In a certain place there was once a viper that used to injure people. They came and told Rabbi Chanina ben Dosa. He said to them, "Show me its hole."

They showed him its hole, and he put his heel over the hole; the viper came out, bit Rabbi Chanina, and died.

Rabbi Chanina put it on his shoulder, brought it to the house of study, and said to them: "See, my sons, it is not the viper that kills, it is sin that kills!"[4]

The residents of a certain place in Israel were feeling threatened by an aggressive viper, and so they reported it to Rabbi Chanina ben Dosa, a first-century scholar who lived in the Galilee in northern Israel, for whom and by whom legend has it many miracles were performed. The rabbi demonstrated to them that it was not the poisonous venom of the viper that was causing injury, but rather it was their sinfulness that was at fault. In other words, the bite was only as dangerous to the victim as the degree to which the person bore sin. When Rabbi Chanina ben Dosa allowed the lizard to bite him, not only was he saved from injury, but the viper itself was killed.

This story suggests that injury or suffering is not the result of specific dangerous circumstances, but rather it is directly linked to inner, personal factors. The same viper can bite two different people; the one bearing sin will succumb to injury, while the one who is not will remain unharmed.

Such an approach sits well with those looking for meaning and explanation in suffering or death. Those who suffer must have sinned,

---

4. Babylonian Talmud, Berachot 33a.

and do not merit God's protection. Those miraculously spared are saved through their deeds or their merits.

It is sin that kills.

Robertson: Sharon's Stroke Is Divine Punishment

On January 4, 2006, Ariel Sharon, the then Prime Minister of the State of Israel, suffered a massive stroke. The next day, it was reported that the American Christian broadcaster Pat Robertson suggested that Sharon's stroke was divine punishment for "dividing God's land."

"God considers this land to be his," Robertson said on his TV program *The 700 Club*. "You read the Bible and he says, 'This is my land,' and for any prime minister of Israel who decides he is going to carve it up and give it away, God says, 'No, this is mine.'"

Robertson said he was very sad to see tragedy befall Sharon, but at the same time, he pointed to the prophecy of Joel as proof that "God has enmity against those who 'divide my land.'"[5]

The sages often emphasized that death is associated with transgression when they told another story involving the ministering angels. In the midrash, the angels are described as challenging God's decision to take the life of Adam, God's first human creation. God responds to their challenge, indicating that Adam died as punishment for his sin, for not following God's command. We assume that this is a reference to his having eaten from the Tree of Knowledge back in the Garden of Eden many, many years earlier. In other words, even though he had reached the age of 930, his death still needed to be justified, there had to be a reason – one did not simply die of old age.[6]

The midrash, however, does not end with God's response. When the ministering angels received their answer regarding the death of Adam, they refocused their attention upon the death of Moses. To strengthen their argument, the midrash records Moses himself making a case for circumventing death:

---

5. Based on the article "Robertson: Sharon's Stroke Is Divine Punishment," USA *Today*, January 5, 2006; available at http://www.usatoday.com/news/nation/2006-01-05-robertson_x.htm.
6. Sifrei, Deuteronomy 339.

COUNTER-TEXT
Moses Was Just Like Everyone Else

"Master of the World! Why do I die?... Is it not better that they should say 'this is Moses who brought us out of Egypt and split the sea for us and brought down the manna for us and performed for us miracles and great deeds' rather than that they should say 'such-and-such *was* Moses, thus-and-thus *did* Moses do'?"

God responded, "Death is a decree from before Me that is equal for all persons."[7]

In other words, God explains to the ministering angels that Moses is not being punished. He has committed no sin worthy of punishment; he is not guilty of any misdeed. Simply put, "his time has come." All human beings die, even though their deaths may cause great inconvenience, or even suffering.

The presentation of these two answers one after the other in the midrash indicates that the sages considered both positions as valid possibilities. That is to say, some people, like Adam, die even at a very old age, as a punishment for their sins. Whatever they did, whenever they did it, they must pay for their transgression through loss of their most precious asset, their very own lives. However others, like Moses, die because that is the way God has set up the world – people are born, and people die. And they may very well die, as in the case of Moses, at the most inopportune moments in life.

People planning to celebrate a joyous occasion – the wedding of their daughter or the bar mitzvah of their son – can find themselves just days before the *simchah* suddenly in a state of mourning. Whether burying a parent, a spouse, a sibling, or a child, they become consumed with the tragedy of the death and then with its catastrophic timing in terms of the *simchah* scheduled to take place in a matter of days. Why did it happen now? What is the meaning, the message?

According to the midrash, there need not be any specific meaning or message. "Death is a decree from before Me that is equal for all persons."[8] Death can happen at any time, without specific connection to the timing.

---

7. Ibid.
8. Ibid.

Looking for Meaning in Suffering

We have established that death may or may not be meaningful. At times, it is the consequence of misdeeds or failure; at other times, it is just the way of the world, a divine decree that no one lives forever.

Then what about suffering? Is adversity always meaningful, always deserved? And in particular, how does one explain the suffering of the righteous (a question we return to a number times throughout this book)? The following texts present differing views on the subject.

TEXT
All Suffering Is Well Deserved

Moses said before Him: Lord of the Universe, why is it that some righteous people prosper and others suffer adversity, some wicked people prosper and others suffer adversity?

The Lord said to Moses: The righteous one who prospers is a perfectly righteous person; the righteous one who suffers is not a perfectly righteous person. The wicked one who prospers is not a perfectly wicked person; the wicked one who suffers is a perfectly wicked person.[9]

Moses asks an eternal question, and gets a very straightforward answer: don't believe everything you see. In other words, although we can only judge the dispositions of people based on what our eyes and ears behold, that is not the whole story. God sees beyond the superficial actions, beyond the skin-deep personality of human beings, beyond their public appearances – into their essence, their secret lives – and rewards or punishes them accordingly. Essentially, according to the Talmud, what we might perceive to be an injustice is only so because we don't see the entire picture. In fact, the righteous individual is not perfectly righteous, the wicked, not perfectly wicked. These inconsistencies are subject to divine judgment, a judgment that will remain beyond our human ability to understand, and may seem unfair and undeserved according to our limited understanding.

God's answer to Moses here is a difficult one. He tells him that all suffering is well deserved, and that all responsibility for what seems unjust in reality lies squarely with the sufferer, not with God. God's judgments are perfect. (A close look at God's answer might still leave us with a glaring question: shouldn't the righteous person who is not perfectly righteous nonetheless be at least

---

9. Babylonian Talmud, Berachot 7a.

as deserving of prosperity as the wicked individual who is not completely wicked? After all, why should a wicked person with a few points in his favor do better in life than a righteous person with a few flaws? Something in this formula needs further explanation! An alternative explanation as to why the wicked prosper will be considered in the next chapter.)

Two generations following the execution of Rabban Shimon ben Gamliel the first, the *nasi* of the Sanhedrin, there lived a rabbi named Rabbi Yannai. In all of Mishnah, the authoritative written collection of hundreds of years of oral law, only one relatively short, yet exceedingly important teaching is recorded in his name. And this teaching presents us with a thought-provoking antithesis to the previous text:

COUNTER-TEXT
We Cannot Explain Suffering
Rabbi Yannai said: It is not in our hands to explain either the contentment of the wicked or the suffering of the righteous.[10]

No doubt Rabbi Yannai knew well of the sufferings of the people in the generations immediately preceding him. He knew of the thousands who had been killed and tortured by the Romans, and by the Greeks that preceded them. And yet, rather than offering understanding, he teaches us here that we have no explanations for such suffering. Rabbeinu Yonah of Gerona (d. 1263, Toledo, Spain) suggested Rabbi Yannai meant to say that though suffering is no doubt meaningful, it will remain one of those things that human beings can never fully fathom.[11] Rabbeinu Yonah points out that even the prophet Jeremiah was frustrated by theodicy, and cried out to God, saying:

> You are always righteous, O Lord,
> when I bring a case before You.
> Yet I would speak with You about Your justice:
> Why does the way of the wicked prosper?
> Why do all the faithless live at ease?[12]

By saying that "it is not in our hands," Yannai acknowledges that there may very well be an explanation, but that we will never be able to grasp it in

---

10. Mishnah Avot 4:19.
11. The commentary of Rabbeinu Yonah on Tractate Avot 4:20. Rabbeinu Yonah was one of the signers of the ban proclaimed in 1233 against Rambam's *Guide for the Perplexed* and the *Sefer HaMadda*.
12. Jeremiah 12:1.

its entirety; it is not humanly possible. However, I would suggest that the straightforward meaning of Rabbi Yannai here is that we just don't know. He is unwilling to conjecture that suffering is always a punishment. He refuses to explain that suffering is well deserved and meaningful.[13] For Yannai, we must live our lives absent of such understanding, without guarantee that just or fair explanations even exist.

Despite Rabbi Yannai's perspective, volumes of rabbinic literature are filled with conjecture as to the meaning of suffering. There is a rather lengthy passage in the Talmud wherein a whole series of statements have been collected, matching specific sins to specific punishments. For example, the Talmud states that as a punishment for the neglect of tithes, the heavens are closed, ceasing to pour down dew and rain, high prices are prevalent, wages are lost, and people pursue a livelihood but they cannot attain. For the crime of robbery, locusts invade, famine is prevalent, and people eat the flesh of their sons and daughters. Also, for the crime of making vain and false oaths, for profaning the Divine Name, and for desecrating Shabbat, wild beasts multiply, (domestic) animals cease, the population decreases, and the roads become desolate.[14]

In reaction to Rabbi Yannai's comments, the contemporary author and renowned teacher Rabbi Benjamin Blech suggested as follows:

> Rabbi Yannai didn't fundamentally disagree with all the other Jewish scholars who preceded him. He wasn't trying to criticize all the rabbis who had offered brilliant insights…. [If that were the case] the Talmud would have followed his comment with the objections of all those who disagreed. No, I am certain that Rabbi Yannai was supportive of every one of these ideas….[15]

Here I strongly disagree with Rabbi Blech. The Talmud exposes us to many different opinions regarding suffering, including Rabbi Yannai's view. The Talmud gives voice to these opposing approaches to explain suffering precisely because there is no one specific Jewish approach to this issue.

---

13. Tiferet Yisrael's comment on this Mishnah suggests that Rabbi Yannai is teaching that there can be multiple reasons for suffering, among them the possibility that the individual caused the suffering to himself by not taking good care of himself.
14. Babylonian Talmud, Shabbat 32a–33b.
15. Benjamin Blech, *If God Is Good, Why Is the World So Bad?* (Deerfield Beach, FL: Simcha Press, 2003), 180–81.

Therefore, believing that there is no rational explanation for suffering is also to be considered a legitimate Jewish belief.

Although according to Rabbi Yannai it is beyond our comprehension, nonetheless, generations upon generations have searched for understanding. In this next text we are taught that, generally speaking, suffering itself has great purpose, thus it is in our best interest to suffer in this world.

TEXT

Give Me Suffering, Give Me Atonement

When Isaac was old…he requested suffering. He said before God: "Master of both worlds! If a man dies without having suffered, the measure of strict judgment is stretched out eternally before him. But if You cause him to suffer, the measure of strict judgment is no longer stretched out eternally before him."

The Holy One, blessed be He, said to him: "By your life, you have requested a good thing! And with you it begins."

So, from the beginning of the Book of Genesis until this point, there is no mention of suffering. But in Isaac's time, God gave him suffering, as it is said, "When Isaac was old and his eyes grew dim (Genesis 27:1)."[16]

According to this midrashic account, we are to understand suffering as something positive. It is a corrective measure that enables us to achieve atonement in this world for our sins, paving the way for a better life in the eternity of the world to come. The midrash is based on the understanding that this world is merely a short preparation for the eternity of the world to come. Therefore, comparatively speaking, the "short-term" suffering that one may experience in this world is well worth experiencing, as it purges us of the sins that may otherwise escort us throughout our everlasting existence in the next world. In other words, suffering in this world should be considered a blessing for which we should be grateful. The following midrash teaches that suffering in this world may even buy us more years of life!

TEXT

Settling the Account

According to the way of the world, a man stumbles by doing a transgression for which [offenders] are liable for death at the

---

16. Genesis Rabbah 65:9.

hands of heaven; [subsequently] his ox dies, his chicken is lost, his plate is shattered, his finger becomes sore, and [by virtue of these many small afflictions] his account is settled.[17]

One more important point should be made here: In the "Isaac midrash" we are taught that human suffering was not a divine initiative, but rather a response to a human prayer, a request that came from none other than our ancestor, Isaac.

God may be the source of our suffering, but it was not His idea.

According to this approach to suffering, human sickness and suffering is to be considered as an antidote, an answer to a passionate prayer for mercy, and ultimately a means for achieving forgiveness for the wrongdoings we inevitably perpetrate in this world.

This then could also serve as an explanation for the imprecise notion regarding the imperfect righteous and the less-than-complete wicked persons referred to in an earlier text in this chapter. The fact that the imperfect righteous person suffers, according to the "Isaac midrash," is actually a benefit to him, for it will serve him well in the world to come. And the borderline wicked person's prosperity is actually going to come back to haunt him in his next-world existence.

This notion is actually spelled out quite clearly in the following Talmudic text:

Just as punishment will be exacted of the wicked in the world to come even for a slight transgression that they commit, so too is punishment exacted in this world of the righteous for any slight transgression that they commit.... Just as the righteous will receive their reward in the world to come, even for the least meritorious act that they do, so too are the wicked rewarded in this world even for the least meritorious act that they do.[18]

Ramban embraces this approach to theodicy. He is convinced that all suffering endured by the righteous in this world is in retribution for their minor transgressions. God sends this adversity in order to maximize the reward awaiting them in the world to come. In contrast, the wicked are given their reward in this world for their few righteous deeds in order to

---

17. Jerusalem Talmud, Sotah 1:7.
18. Babylonian Talmud, Taanit 11a.

maximize their suffering in the afterlife. Ramban cites the teaching of the School of Rabbi Yishmael[19] that anyone for whom forty days have passed without *yisurin* (slight sufferings or inconveniences) should beware, for that person has received his reward already in this world, and will have nothing but suffering awaiting him in the world to come.[20] Rabbeinu Yonah, in his commentary to Pirkei Avot, also expressed the opinion that suffering is meant as a punishment in this world to better prepare us for the world to come.[21]

However, there is another tradition that holds us responsible for the presence of sickness and suffering in our world, albeit for a very different reason. This view bases itself upon the actions of a different ancestor, Jacob.

COUNTER-TEXT

A Chance to Say Good-Bye

Until the time of Jacob, there was no infirmity, and then Jacob prayed to God [that he be granted infirmity], and infirmity came into being, as it says: And it was said unto Joseph, "Behold, your father is ill (Genesis 48:1)."[22]

Why, we ask ourselves, would anyone pray for infirmity? Is it for the same reason that Isaac, Jacob's father, had yearned for suffering, a type of indemnity preparing for the world to come?

In his commentary on this passage of the Talmud, Rashi (1040–1105) provides a powerful insight and explanation.[23] He suggests that Jacob had a very different practical concern. He was concerned that each of his sons would have sufficient warning to be able to travel from their homes and be with him at the time of his death. It is for this reason, says Rashi, that Jacob prayed for infirmity. A separate midrash teaches us that prior to Jacob, a person might just sneeze and die immediately (thus the widespread custom of saying "God bless you" when hearing someone sneeze).[24] To die instantly like that leaves a family without the opportunity to say good-bye. (This is the case when death occurs suddenly amid traumatic circumstances.)

---

19. Babylonian Talmud, Arachin 16b.
20. Ramban, "Torat HaAdam," in *Kitvei HaRamban*, ed. Haim Chavel (Jerusalem: Mossad HaRav Kook, 1988), 2:281.
21. Commentary of Rabbeinu Yonah on Mishnah Avot, 3:16, s.v. "*vehakol*."
22. Babylonian Talmud, Sanhedrin 107b.
23. Ibid.
24. Midrash Yalkut Shimoni, Parashat Lech Lecha, 77.

With the introduction of infirmity, upon hearing that a beloved relative is on his deathbed, close relatives and friends are given the opportunity to come and be with the stricken one. They have the opportunity to say one last good-bye. This was so critical to Jacob that he requested infirmity in order to be blessed with just such an opportunity.

Whether or not this is an etiological myth about the origins of infirmity prior to death need not concern us. What is important is that this particular rabbinic story suggests an alternative basis for frailty and suffering prior to death. Such a condition is not necessarily the result of misdeeds or transgressions. We are taught that Jacob suffered infirmity not because he deserved it, but rather because it gave him a chance to ponder his mortality and gather his thoughts concerning what he wanted to address to each of his children, what legacy he wanted to leave each one them.

When a Suicide Bomber Took Kinneret Boosany's Physical Beauty, She Found the Beauty Inside

Kinneret Boosany had been a waitress in a Tel Aviv restaurant called My Coffee Shop when a Palestinian suicide bomber chose it as his target. It was March 30, 2002, at 9:30 in the evening.

She says a young guy came in and asked for a cup of coffee. That's the last thing she remembers. When she regained consciousness it was July, four months later.

She had survived the attack, which killed one other woman, but just barely. She had burns on 70 percent of her body, her dominant left arm burned most severely. She lost the sight in her right eye and her lung capacity was reduced by half.

Despite the severity of her injuries, Boosany says there was never a time when she wished she had not survived the blast.

"Never," she says. "For the whole time I was in a coma I was struggling to live."

In fact, she calls the threshold between death and life a holy place – because that's where she feels she discovered a critical truth about her existence.

"The first time you wake up you say, 'thank God I'm alive...' That's all that matters. But the farther you get from the danger of death, you get more confused because the pressure of the material world begins to affect you again," she says. "You've been in a place much more holy because you only survived to live. You don't care if you have legs. No legs, no eyes, no skin – you don't care. As long as I'm alive, that's what matters. But when you start coming back to reality, which unfortunately is 'worship the money, worship the body,' it becomes more confusing. You start asking yourself questions, how will I manage the house, how will I find a partner?"

For her, recovery meant years of surgery and rehabilitation. She has needed skin grafts, repairs and cosmetic work, requiring 14 operations so far….

"I can tell you I am more happy now with the person I am today than I was before the bombing. There is more peace, more calm. There's less need to look around for stuff elsewhere. Now if I feel a lack of something I know I need to go into me – it's all inside. A lot of problems that I used to have then, I don't have them anymore. You know that you can get through anything…."

"This is my lesson that God sent me," she says. "It has nothing to do with the Israeli-Palestinian conflict…. Kinneret got burned. Kinneret died actually. Kinneret Haya was born."[25]

The story of Kinneret Boosany is very powerful. It no doubt takes a lot of introspection to recast one's personal suffering as a gift from God, an opportunity to rethink one's personal values. In fact, it's an inspiration.

One of the great American rabbinic leaders of the twentieth century, Joseph B. Soloveitchik, gave a lot of thought to the issue of faith related to suffering. In one of his essays, he wrote:

> Afflictions come to elevate a person, to purify and sanctify his spirit, to cleanse and purge it of the dross of superficiality and vulgarity, to refine his soul and to broaden his horizons. In a word, the function of suffering is to mend that which is flawed in an individual's personality.[26]

---

25. Original version of this story published on the Yahoo! News website, Kevin Sites in the Hot Zone, on February 9, 2006. An expanded version can be found in the book *In the Hot Zone: One Man, One Year, Twenty Wars*, published by Harper Perennial October 2007.
26. Joseph B. Soloveitchik, "Kol Dodi Dofek," in *Theological and Halachic Reflections on the Holocaust*, ed. B.H. Rosenberg (Hoboken, NJ: Ktav Publishing House, 1992), 56.

Jacob longed for infirmity, to give him time to prepare his legacy. He saw it as a means to an end. Kinneret found meaning in her own tragedy, and she too has used it as a means to an end.

We now have two different viewpoints on suffering – one related to Isaac and the other related to Jacob. Taken together, they lead us to the conclusion that illness or suffering may or may not be for the sake of atonement. It seems that on the one hand, a person may choose to see his suffering as deserved, as a mechanism for purging him of his worldly sins; but on the other hand, he may choose to see his suffering as an opportunity, offering him a practical opportunity to live differently, or to contribute to the enrichment of the lives of others. However, what both of these approaches have in common is the notion that the suffering is sent by God, for a specific purpose. This is the salient message of the words of Rabbi Yose ben Yehudah as well, who said, "Precious are sufferings, for the name of the Omnipresent rests upon the one to whom sufferings come."[27]

"Their Souls Had a Job to Do and They Were Finished"

On March 22, 2005, Philyss Seidenfeld lost four of her seven children in a horrible Teaneck fire. In the months since, Seidenfeld has inspired her friends with the strength of her belief, which has enabled her to cope with her tragedy. "It was God's will," she said. "Their souls had a job to do and they were finished."

The extent of Seidenfeld's recovery has been remarkable. She suffered severe burns to her respiratory system and was hooked up to a respirator for a full week following the fire. Doctors expected an intensive six-week recovery period, but after only three weeks Seidenfeld rose from bed, her life invigorated with renewed significance. "I was spared for a reason," she said. "Now, more than ever, my life has a purpose."

Since the tragedy, Seidenfeld has committed herself to helping people find faith amid the challenge of crisis. Just as she was miraculously spared in the fire, she urges people to find the blessing in their lives and crises. "Suffering should not be seen as punishment, but as an invitation to initiate an intimate conversation with God," she said.

---

27. Sifrei, Deuteronomy 32.

Seidenfeld's faith has enabled her to look positively even at the deaths of her children. "They're with God now. They're in a perpetual state of eternal bliss. They did what they needed to do and reached spiritual perfection. They're settled. What more could a mother ask for?"[28]

Does our tradition demand that each and every one of us who suffers embark upon an inner journey to find meaning in our suffering? Is this what is expected of us? Need there always be meaning?

The texts we turn to now take us into the world of the great sage Rabbi Yochanan ben Nappacha, who lived in the land of Israel during the third century CE. He is revealed to us here during a specific period in his life when he was dealing with physical suffering, both personally as well as that of others. Once again, varying texts describing that period in his life will leave us with conflicting approaches to the meaning of suffering.

TEXT
Suffering of the Pious Is a Test from God

Rabbi Yochanan was sick, becoming ill with chills for three and a half years. Rabbi Chanina went up to visit him. He said to him: "What is on your mind?"

He replied: "[My suffering] is more than I can bear."

He said to him: "Don't say this, rather say, '[This is from] the faithful God.'"

When his pain became greater he would say, "[This is from] the faithful God." But when his pain became too great for him, Rabbi Chanina went up to him, recited a word [an incantation] over him, and he was relieved.

After some days, Rabbi Chanina became ill. Rabbi Yochanan went up to visit him. He said to him: "What is on your mind?"

Rabbi Chanina replied: "How difficult are my sufferings!"

Rabbi Yochanan said to him: "But how great is their reward!"

Rabbi Chanina replied: "I want neither them nor their reward."

Rabbi Yochanan said to him: "Why don't you recite that word that you recited over me and heal yourself?"

---

28. Based on the article by Deena Yellin, "Sustained by Faith: Mother of Fire Victims Sees Way to Honor Them," *The Record*, March 10, 2006.

Rabbi Chanina replied: "When I was outside, I could be responsible for others, but while I am inside, do I not need others to be responsible for me?"

Rabbi Yochanan said to him: "'My beloved is mine, and I am his, that feeds among the lilies' (Song of Songs 2:16). The rod of the Holy One, blessed be He, only seeks out and sets down upon one whose heart is soft as a lily."[29]

The notion of suffering as a test from God is well entrenched in our Jewish worldview. Beginning with our study of the Tanach, we have been taught to understand the suffering of our ancestors as purposeful, as sent by God for a reason. Our matriarchs suffered from barrenness, our patriarchs from life-threatening encounters with enemies from without and from within, there was famine, there was imprisonment and slavery. We have been taught to understand these sufferings as tests from the Almighty Whose love for us means at times that He will test us or chastise us in order to fine-tune our behaviors, in order to make us into better human beings, to make us even more worthy of the blessings and rewards He has in store for His faithful ones.

This seems to be the clear message that Rabbi Yochanan teaches us in this midrashic passage. After suffering for nearly four years, and reaching a point where he felt that his suffering was more than he could bear, he is blessed with a visit from a colleague who enables him to put his suffering into perspective, thereby finding greater strength to endure. Rabbi Chanina empowers Rabbi Yochanan to appreciate that because the suffering comes from God, Who is faithful and equitable, rather than complain he should learn to accept that his suffering is meaningful. Rabbi Yochanan seems to have taken to heart this important insight, and it is reported that he was able to deal with even greater pain than before. However, there does come a time where physically he is unable to endure further pain, and therefore, Rabbi Chanina comes to him and relieves him of his pain through the use of a mystical incantation. We are to understand that this is something Rabbi Chanina could have done earlier, but since suffering is from God, for a purpose that God alone knows is good for us, Rabbi Chanina holds back taking away his colleague's pain. For, in the greater scheme of things, it would be doing a disservice to Rabbi Yochanan.

When the tables are turned, and it is Rabbi Chanina who is suffering, Rabbi Yochanan comes to his aid. He must now be strong for Rabbi Chanina,

---

29. Shir HaShirim Rabbah 2:16.

and so he demonstrates through his words that he was a good student. Now it is Rabbi Yochanan's responsibility to encourage his colleague/teacher, and he does so by sharing with him a different insight into suffering.

If the reward is not appealing, he seems to say, then accept the suffering as an indication that you are among the righteous. For God only brings suffering upon those whose heart is gentle and pliant enough to accept it with love, as God's incomprehensible decree from upon high. In other words, God only tests those who are righteous, and therefore, the one who suffers should take comfort in knowing that God has designated him as one of those righteous ones, and that itself should serve as an inspiration.

Rabbi Chanina's startling response, "Neither them nor their reward," coming on the heels of his earlier stance of acceptance, still requires clarification. A different account of Rabbi Yochanan, his own suffering, and the suffering he confronts in others, may help explain Rabbi Chanina's position.

COUNTER-TEXT
Give Me Your Hand

Rabbi Chiya bar Abba fell ill and Rabbi Yochanan went in to visit him. He said to him: "Are your sufferings welcome to you?"

He replied: "Neither them nor their reward."

He said to him: "Give me your hand." He gave him his hand and he raised him.

Rabbi Yochanan once fell ill and Rabbi Chanina went in to visit him. He said to him: "Are your sufferings welcome to you?"

He replied: "Neither them nor their reward."

He said to him: "Give me your hand." He gave him his hand and he raised him.

Why could not Rabbi Yochanan raise himself? They replied: "The prisoner cannot free himself from prison."[30]

The account of Rabbi Yochanan's experience with suffering is told very differently in this version. Setting aside the possible socio-historic reasons for these differences (that is, differences between the cultures affecting Jewish life in the countries where these two texts were written down), we will consider the differences at face value, recognizing the significantly different approach to the experience of suffering that is being conveyed here by the very same rabbinic figures.

---

30. Babylonian Talmud, Berachot 5b.

Our text begins with Rabbi Yochanan visiting his sick colleague, Rabbi Chiya. Recognizing Chiya's suffering to be unwanted, he does not look for ways to encourage Chiya to find meaning, or to be accepting or comforted. Instead, he goes right to work, taking Chiya's hand and providing him with relief from his suffering.

Immediately, the scene shifts to the occasion we read about in the previous midrash, when Rabbi Yochanan was sick and Rabbi Chanina came to visit him. In this account, Chanina asks Yochanan whether he wants to continue to suffer, and Yochanan, like Chiya, answers flat out, "No, I don't want the suffering, and I don't want the reward." And here, without incantations or apologies that attempt to help the sufferer find meaning in his lot, Chanina does just what Yochanan did for Chiya – he gives him his hand and provides with relief from his suffering.

This second rendition of the suffering of these great sages supports the legitimacy of protest in the face of suffering. That is to say, there is no special merit to accepting one's suffering, neither as a test from God nor as a means of reaping special rewards. In addition, one is not obligated to seek explanations. For this reason, in each case here the sufferer is asked if it is his preference to seek meaning, to anticipate reward. This is a personal choice, and a legitimate one for the individual who is so motivated. However, the text teaches that while this remains an option, it is not a requirement nor is it necessarily a preferred approach to dealing with suffering.

What does the narrator mean to tell us when he says that the visitor "gave him his hand and he raised him"? What is the meaning of this expression? While some commentators again seek to understand this as a mystical power to heal, harnessed by these sagacious rabbis, I wish to suggest a different reading of the story.

When we suffer, we have been conditioned to see our suffering as God's will; God has sent this suffering upon us for a reason. This is the way that suffering is presented in the text above. When we are in the midst of physical or emotional anguish, we cannot think rationally. Knowing that one approach to suffering is to assume it is meaningful, we can easily become obsessed with blaming ourselves for our suffering or looking for justifications of all sorts. When this course is therapeutic, it is considered acceptable. However, when it becomes obsessive, it is counterproductive and self-destructive.

When we are the victims, locked inside our suffering and obsessed with finding a reason for it, we need the level-headedness of another human being, someone to come along and remind us that our pursuit of meaning in suffering is not a requirement. It is normal for people to assume there is a reason, that there is a way of logically answering the question "What did I do to deserve this?" However, in addition to the trauma of the suffering, the sufferer may be prone to compound his suffering in his search for a satisfactory answer to this question.

Under such circumstances, it may very well take an outsider to come along and help us to climb out of our obsession. We need the warm hand of another human being to remind us that we do not deserve to suffer, we did not bring it upon ourselves, and we need not continue to dwell on that possibility. That friend or loved one can help us to rise up out of this dimension of our suffering, which compounds our misery with a combination of guilt and anxiety.

Should we be in need of such comfort, then we are taught that we are under no obligation to look for meaning in our suffering, nor to appreciate it and anticipate reward. We are permitted to guiltlessly let go of the possibility of all such explanations or interpretations, and simply look forward to better days ahead.

The continuation of this counter-text makes this point quite clear:

Rabbi Elazar fell ill and Rabbi Yochanan went in to visit him. He noticed that he was lying in a dark room, and he bared his arm and light radiated from it. Thereupon he noticed that Rabbi Elazar was weeping, and he said to him: "Why do you weep?

"Is it because you did not study enough Torah? Surely we learned: 'The one who sacrifices much and the one who sacrifices little have the same merit, provided that the heart is directed to heaven' (Mishnah Menachot 13:11).

"Is it perhaps lack of sustenance? Not everybody has the privilege to enjoy two tables [spiritual and material wealth].

"Is it perhaps because of [the lack of] children? This is the bone of my tenth son!"

Rabbi Elazar replied to him: "I am weeping on account of this beauty that is going to rot in the earth." [Rabbi Yochanan was known to be quite handsome.]

Rabbi Yochanan replied: "On that account you surely have a reason to weep," and they both wept.

In the meanwhile Rabbi Yochanan said to him: "Are your sufferings welcome to you?"

Rabbi Elazar replied: "Neither them nor their reward."

Rabbi Yochanan said to him: "Give me your hand," and he gave him his hand and he raised him.[31]

When the same Rabbi Yochanan visits Rabbi Elazar in the midst of the latter's suffering, he seeks to bring him comfort. Upon seeing Rabbi Elazar crying, he assumes that he is crying out of guilt over his sinful actions.

Assessing the situation in this way, Rabbi Yochanan launches into a text-based logical refutation of such a notion.

For instance, if Rabbi Elazar feels that he must blame his personal suffering on not reaching his potential in terms of the quantity of Torah he studied in his lifetime (a common assumption among the rabbis of the Talmudic times, and in our times as well), then Rabbi Yochanan reminds him of the rabbinic teaching that states that quantity is not essential, but rather what is most important is quality, that one has the right intentions. In other words, quantity of Torah is not punishable.

Wealth is just luck, he says, and not having children is not a punishment either. To support this contention, he shows Rabbi Elazar a bone of his tenth child, as if to say, "I myself have had ten children, and buried ten children, and I refuse to understand it as punishment – therefore, you need not see your childlessness as a punishment either."

After all of these arguments, Rabbi Elazar indicates that indeed none of the issues just raised are troubling him. He then shares with Rabbi Yochanan his real concern, the point that has brought him to tears. Pointing to Rabbi Yochanan's handsome physical appearance, he said to him, "I am crying on account of this beauty that will rot in the earth."

Hearing these words, Rabbi Yochanan commiserates and replies, "For this you should surely cry." And the two of them cried together.

Strange as the conclusion to this Talmudic tale may seem at first reading, its message is quite poignant. Rabbi Elazar, like Rabbi Yochanan, refuses to view his suffering and possible death as a punishment or atonement for past sins or shortcomings. This is not the reason for his melancholy. Rather,

---

31. Ibid.

he weeps for the ultimate demise of all living things, of all the miracles and splendor that accompany our lives on this earth. Perhaps Rabbi Elazar's own suffering reminded him of human mortality in general. The beautiful material blessings of our lives, those that surround us for the years we are privileged to live here, must all come to an end. We may weep for and mourn the loss of the blessings we have in our lives, the blessings that come and go from generation to generation, but there is no reason to see such unavoidable loss as purposeful. There is no need to assume that it is guilt or sin that has decreed these sufferings upon us. We are not required to conjecture, accept explanations, or search for meaning in the midst of our pain. Of course there is reason to be sorrowful, but it is the mournful grief of lost life, wisdom, beauty, and love, not the regret of past sins and their punishments, that need bring all of us to tears.

The handsome Rabbi Yochanan commiserates with his colleague. And then, as he had done for Rabbi Chiya and Rabbi Chanina had done for him, he clarifies if it is Rabbi Elazar's intention to search for meaning in this suffering. When he replies in the negative, Rabbi Yochanan reaches out to him to help him through the suffering, to relieve his anguish, to empathize with his pain, and ultimately to enable his healing.

The desire to find meaning and understanding amid suffering is identified by the rabbis as a very normal human reaction. What we learn from the variety of stories and teachings, and especially from the varying renderings of the very same story, is that we have in our tradition more than one appropriate Jewish response to suffering. For those who find the search for meaning in suffering important, and pursue an answer to the questions "What did I do to deserve this?" or "What is the meaning of my suffering?" there are texts that attest to the appropriateness of such a quest. One may conclude that one's suffering is the result of sin, or that it has come about to provide atonement in this world and open the door for greater reward in the next. Perhaps it comes to provide opportunity to settle accounts, to make peace and bring about closure.

On the other hand, for those who choose otherwise, for those who refuse to assume that their personal suffering is meaningful or that is has been decreed from on high, they too will find rabbinic traditions in support of their preference. Even death, which happens eventually to everyone, can occur in the most inconvenient of times for those who are left behind, without bearing a specific meaning or message.

Chapter 3

BUT ISN'T EVERYTHING GOD'S DECREE?

On January 19, 2006, an Islamic Jihad suicide bomber blew himself up at a Tel Aviv fast-food stand, the Rosh Ha'ir Shawarma Restaurant, wounding twenty people. Blood, shattered glass, and debris covered the ground. The windows of a parked car were blown out, and helmeted security forces cordoned off the area.

> "All of a sudden, there was an explosion. I looked out and I saw people running with blood on them," said Benny Ezrami, who works at a trinket store next door. His co-worker, Maya Hazfon, said, "God protected us."[1]

Just under three months later, on April 17, 2006, eleven people were killed and over sixty wounded in a suicide bombing at the very same restaurant in Tel Aviv. Once again, the Islamic Jihad claimed responsibility for the attack.

When Daniel Wultz, a sixteen-year-old teenager, died one month later of his wounds from that attack, the family's rabbi recalled visiting Daniel in the hospital just after the attack:

> "I saw him wake up and open his eyes for the first time – there was such emotion, such wonderful hope that God would listen favorably to our prayers," he said. "The whole community was praying for his recovery, but God wanted something different."[2]

In a video released by the group, the bomber said the bombing was dedicated to the thousands of Palestinian prisoners in Israeli jails:

1. "Suicide Blast Wounds 20 in Tel Aviv," Associated Press, January 19, 2006; http://www.msnbc.msn.com/id/10923135/from/RL.2/.
2. Talya Halkin, "People Here Are Left Speechless," *Jerusalem Post*, May 15, 2006; http://www.jpost.com/servlet/Satellite?cid=1145961342826&pagename=JPArticle%2FShowFull.

"I carry out this operation in response to the massacres committed by the Zionist enemy against our people and brothers in the West Bank and Gaza," he said in the video. "There will be more such operations with the will of God."[3]

In the ongoing conflict in the Middle East, God is brought into the conflict on all sides. He is given credit for the miraculous salvation of the near-victims, considered responsible for the deaths of the fatally wounded, and cited as the inspiration for the ongoing violence by the terrorists.

Politics aside, is God working in support of both sides of the Middle East conflict? Is it all God's will – the miracles, the deaths, and the endless violence? If God doesn't want the conflict to continue, then can't He put a stop to it?

When a terrorist achieves his goal, is that God's will? When certain people are miraculously spared, and others are seriously wounded, maimed, horribly disfigured, or killed – is all of this the will of God as well? Is everything that happens, every detail, to be accepted as the direct result of God's divine decree?

On March 21, 2002, a suicide bombing on King George Street in Jerusalem killed three people and injured eighty-seven. Avraham Bauer and his seven-year-old son, Yehonathon, were injured in the attack, Yehonathon quite seriously. In an interview, Avraham was asked if he ever asks God why his family deserved to go through this experience.

> [Avraham] thinks for several moments, then replies: "In any situation such as this, you ask, 'Why did this happen?' And you can answer it in one of three ways. The first answer is, 'It was a random event. I was in the wrong place at the wrong time.' The second is, 'It happened because of terrorists; terrorists have the power to hurt people.'
>
> "Now, if you believe either of these two, you're repudiating the Torah. The Torah is full of *pesukim* [passages] that [say] there is no such thing as chance, and that there is nothing separate from Hashem. Would anyone say, 'Hashem was out having coffee when this happened'? And if you believe that the terrorists possess power independent of Hashem's Will, you're denying *hashgachah pratit* [divine providence], and that Hashem is One.

---

3. "Suicide Bomber Kills Nine in Tel Aviv," Associated Press, April 17, 2006; http://www.msnbc.msn.com/id/12351695/.

"There's only one other possibility: that everything is from Hashem and Hashem is only good. Everything evil in the world is under Hashem's total control. The Ramchal writes this, and a person has to see this very clearly, that all is controlled by Hakadosh Boruch Hu. Even though we may not understand it, this is the foundation: that everything that happens is for the good. Even though it was very painful, and we did a lot of crying, what we went through was only from Yad Hashem [the Hand of God]. On this, there was never a moment of doubt."[4]

Sin and Suffering

According to one theory, stated here by Rav Ammi, every instance of suffering or death is to be attributed to sin. The innocent do not suffer.

TEXT

All Suffering and Death Is Divine Punishment for Sin

Rav Ammi said: There is no death without sin, and there is no suffering without guilt.

There is no death without sin, for it is written, "The soul that sins, it will die: the son will not bear the guilt of his father, nor will the father bear the guilt of his son, the righteousness of the righteous will be upon him, and the wickedness of the wicked will be upon him" (Ezekiel 18:20).

There is no suffering without guilt, for it is written, "Then will I respond to their transgression with the rod, and their guilt with the whip" (Psalms 89:33).[5]

Based on this approach, every victim of terror, every casualty of war, every death or maiming that has resulted from a plane crash or an automobile accident was deserved and decreed by God.

Wouldn't that mean that a terrorist attack that takes the lives of a dozen people is also being carried out through God's bidding?

---

4. Sarah Shapiro, "Feeling the Hand of God," *Jewish Action* 68, no. 2 (winter 5768/2008), 39. Printed by permission of the author.
5. Babylonian Talmud, Shabbat 55a.

Is God in Control?

On September 11, 2001 millions of people watched in horror as the second plane crashed into the World Trade Center. Why did God allow it to happen? Many were praying for God to protect their loved ones. And yet they watched the horrible destruction occur. Many people asked questions. Why did this happen? Did God not love those people in the towers and in the planes? Did God not have the power to stop it? Christians would certainly say he had the power to prevent it. But he chose not to. Some might point to one or two cases in which God supposedly did intervene. I have heard of a flight attendant who woke up sick that morning, and called to say she could not make it to work. Later, her plane crashed into the World Trade Center. That is a nice story. But I keep thinking – what about the attendant that took her place? Was God not protecting him or her?

What about the thousands that died that day? Where was God's protection? I've heard the recurring response: "Perhaps God had some mysterious purpose in letting them die, or perhaps their time on earth was done." Some would even tell me he allowed it to punish the people in those planes, or to punish their nation. We are told that God – who has reasons we do not understand – worked his own plans. But I find that unbelievable. Imagine the details that God would have had to control to assure that only those people whose time had come were killed. What if the planes had hit several stories higher or lower? What if the flights had been delayed 10 minutes? What if somebody in the towers had gotten stuck in traffic that morning? What if the planes had hit at a different angle? What if the North Tower had collapsed first? All of these things would have altered the death toll. If God had planned for certain people to die that day, then he must have guided all of these details. He must have guided the planes to hit the buildings exactly where they did.

In other words, God would have had to have been in control of those airplanes, and the terrorists were merely doing what God directed.[6]

---

6. Merle Hertzler, "Questioning: An Examination of Christian Belief." Printed with author's permission.

According to such an approach, we might extrapolate that when a suicide bomber blows himself up in a crowded restaurant in Tel Aviv, the determining factor that decides who will live and who will die is not in the hands of the bomber, but rather, it is a function of the sins or merits of each and every potential victim. Those who are spared can assume that they have experienced a miracle. On some level, their merits have protected them from injury and suffering, and God's recognition of these merits has served to redeem them.

However, the Talmud continues. It cites a teaching that lists a number of biblical figures, such as Benjamin the son of Jacob, and Amram the father of Moses, who, according to tradition, did not sin. Following the incident of the serpent and the eating from the Tree of Knowledge in the Garden of Eden, death became an inevitable end for all living beings. These biblical figures only died because of that incident. And therefore, the Talmudic sages conclude as follows:

COUNTER-TEXT
Suffering and Death Are Not Necessarily God's Decree
We see that there is suffering without sin, there is death without transgression.[7]

Rav Ammi's teaching, that all death and suffering is punishment for sin, decreed of God, is not presented as the final word on the matter. Rather, the Talmud here counters with a proof indicating there isn't necessarily a direct relationship between sin and death or sin and suffering. In an effort to make sense of this, Blech writes the following:

> Where is the justice of God when the perfect die? [The rabbis'] answer is profound in its simplicity. In a perfect world, in the Garden of Eden, Adam and Eve should have lived forever. But once the world has become corrupt and is no longer a paradise because of the people in it, then everyone must die, *especially* the good people. This imperfect world is just not good enough for people who are perfect.... And this is why we can now have death without sin, not as punishment but as deserved reward.[8]

---

7. Babylonian Talmud, Shabbat 55b.
8. Blech, *If God Is Good*, 64–65.

Is this what the Talmudic sages meant to teach us? Note that they not only relate to "death without transgression," but also to "suffering without sin." How does the "deserved reward" thesis fit the phenomena of what seems to be a world filled with unjust suffering?

It is a mistake to read into this Talmudic passage more than it is saying. The statement is not coming to explain anything – it is strictly coming as an observation, an admission that there are those in this world who suffer or die having committed no sin. The Talmud does not suggest that their suffering or death is purposeful! In fact, it is the Talmud's silence here that betrays its powerful message. It presents us with an important, forgotten Jewish tradition that wishes to convey a simple yet difficult lesson: suffering and death are parts of human existence, without any particular divine justification. Suffering and death can be manifestations of God's will…but not necessarily.

Let's consider another approach to explaining suffering. Spanish Jewish philosopher Rabbi Yehudah HaLevi (1075–1141) claimed that all that happens to us in the world falls into one of four categories:

> All phenomena are either *divine*, *natural*, by *chance*, or the result of *choice*.
>
> *Divine* phenomena are those that emanate directly from God and cannot be averted….
>
> *Natural* phenomena occur through intermediary causes specially prepared for these phenomena, and which bring these phenomena to their intended fruition….
>
> *Incidental* phenomena…occur by *chance*, not naturally, not in an organized fashion, nor intentionally….
>
> *Chosen* phenomena are the result of human will, occurring when one makes a decision…. The soul is positioned between the choice and its counter-choice. It is able to choose whichever it desires.[9]

How can God, Who is wholly good and all-powerful, allow for the existence of undeserved, purposeless suffering or death, the result of mere *chance* or as a consequence of *human choice*?

---

9. *Kuzari*, Essay 5, Principle 10, 20:8–11. Italics in all citations from the *Kuzari* are my own.

Admittedly, the idea that certain incidents happen *by chance*, or more specifically as the result of *human choice*, and not as a product of God's direct will, is not easily integrated into many people's faith-systems. However, it does enable HaLevi to explain a difficult point that we considered in our previous chapter.

When the wicked prosper, the Talmud suggests[10] that it is a sign that they are not "wholly wicked," leaving us to wonder why it is that a righteous person who isn't "wholly righteous" should have to suffer any more than an evil person who isn't "wholly evil." Why does the latter prosper at all? Suggests HaLevi:

> The good that comes about through incidental [and natural] phenomena is not withheld from wicked people, and certainly not from saintly people. *This is the reason why the wicked prosper –* they are the beneficiaries of these incidental and natural causes, and there is nothing to prevent them from occurring.[11]

Let's consider for a moment the potential results of believing that everything – absolutely everything that happens in our world – is the result of God's will. While for many this notion may bolster faith, in certain situations it may lead to great doubt.

The summer of 2005 marked the end of an era in modern Israeli history with the unilateral withdrawal from the Gaza strip. Twenty-one Israeli settlements in Gaza plus four more in the West Bank were evacuated; more than nine thousand Israeli citizens were removed from their homes in the course of just a few days. Emotions ran high leading up to the disengagement. Many faithful residents believed that a miracle was on the horizon, that God would not let this happen; Jews would not evict Jews from their homes.

But they were wrong. It happened.

Immediately after the evacuation, P. (an anonymous former resident of Gaza), age twenty-one, began to rebel against Orthodox practice. A self-proclaimed "religious girl, a product of ulpana [religious high school for girls]" prior to disengagement, P. smoked a cigarette on Shabbat one month after. She explains her attitude as follows:

10. Babylonian Talmud, Berachot 7a.
11. *Kuzari*, Essay 1, Principle 10, 20:25.

I felt very disappointed. I really believed God wouldn't do this, then He did. I felt very angry – at the State, at everything, at God. If God is all good and all powerful, yet could do something like this and hurt us in such a way, then I don't have a conscience anymore…. Every time I get on a bus on Shabbat and get these bouts of conscience and ask myself, "Why are you doing this?" I answer: "God hurt me much more."[12]

From this real-life example, we see how an acute belief in the idea that God is directing everything that happens in our lives, and that everything we experience is a direct result of His will, can lead to great disillusionment for the person who experiences inexplicable injustice in his/her personal life. Not everyone can suffer so and keep their faith together with the belief that "everything is for the good" or that "God has a purpose for everything He does."

On the other hand, believing that suffering can happen by mere "chance" leads directly to the agonizing question of God's role in a world where there exists meaningless suffering.

At this point, we are not quite ready to suggest answers to this challenging question. Suffice it to say that although this tradition too is accompanied by its serious theological challenges, it is, nonetheless, a bona fide Jewish tradition.

For those who find this alternate tradition difficult to accept, know that you are in good company. One great medieval scholar, Rabbi Menachem Meiri (1249–1310), bothered so by the literal understanding of the above Talmudic text and the implications of such an approach, wrote the following:

It is one of the foundation principles of Judaism to believe that God determines all that happens to a person – both the good and the bad – according to the person's deeds. One should not be confused by what seems to contradict this principle, i.e., the suffering of the righteous and the pleasures of the wicked. It seems that the righteous and wicked are treated the same. In fact, the nature of justice is hidden from us and we don't know why a particular person is punished or is rewarded. We

––––––––––––
12. *Jerusalem Post*, April 27, 2007.

do know the general principle that God does not withhold the compensation due to any creature – whether pleasure or punishment. This principle is what our sages meant when they said, "There is no death without sin and there is no suffering without transgression."

Do not be disturbed by the fact that this principle is apparently refuted in the Talmud when it says that four died by the sin of the serpent – thus indicating that death is a universal punishment because of the serpent and was implanted in Nature. It should not be taken literally because we know that there is no one who hasn't sinned. Furthermore, even though the Talmud appears to reject the principle that death and suffering is caused by sin, since it uses the term *tiyuvta* [a contradiction based on a *beraita*] – that conclusion is incorrect. This is because our religious beliefs are not dependent upon proofs from the simple meaning of verses and aggadah. There is the established principle that one does not resolve issues entirely on the basis of aggadah. The fact is that even Moses and Aaron died because of their sins, and obviously so has everyone else.[13]

Risks and Righteousness

In chapter 1 we discussed Elisha ben Avuyah, who considered that his fate was sealed when he expressed doubt in divine justice. We read there of a case where a person involved in a mitzvah that promises long life, the shooing away of the mother bird before taking its eggs, fell from a tree to his death while in the midst of fulfilling this commandment. In another Talmudic passage, a similar event is further analyzed by the rabbis. A child had followed his father's instructions[14] – he had climbed the tree, shooed away the mother bird, and taken the eggs – and he was on his way down the ladder when he tragically fell to his death.

How can actions such as this end so catastrophically? The individual was involved in the simultaneous fulfillment of two biblical commandments, both of them promising a long life to the one who diligently fulfills them! How could such an accident have happened?

---

13. Meiri, *Beit HaBechirah*, commentary on Babylonian Talmud, Shabbat 55a.
14. Another Torah commandment that carries with it the promise of long life. See Exodus 20:12.

TEXT
Miracles and Rickety Ladders

Rabbi Elazar asked: "Those who are on the way to perform a commandment are never harmed! So how did this come about?"

One could answer that when they are on their way to fulfill the commandment, it is different. Here, he had completed the fulfillment of the commandment and he was only on his return when he fell to his death.

But no, Rabbi Elazar actually stated: "Those who are engaged in the fulfillment of a commandment are never harmed, neither when going nor returning!"

Rather, it was a rickety ladder, so that injury was likely, and where injury is likely one must not rely on a miracle.[15]

This text exposes us to an important idea. It seems that there are circumstances in our lives when miracles are preempted by dangerous conditions. That is to say that even those who are deserving of divine protection, even those in the midst of fulfilling one or more of God's commandments, will not be spared.

Why should a "rickety ladder" be a challenge for God? What is the underlying message of this text?

The rabbis teach that when it comes to taking certain types of risks, one can expect that God will protect us:

COUNTER-TEXT
The Lord Protects the Unwary

Since the multitudes are accustomed to it, "the Lord protects the unwary" (Psalms 116:6).[16]

The notion conveyed here is that any activity routinely undertaken by people and not perceived by them to be hazardous is permitted despite the inherent danger. To the extent that a person is found worthy, divine providence (*hashgacha pratit*) is extended to the "unwary" – those who choose to engage in such activities without regard for the inherent potential danger.

Of course, to willfully commit a daredevil act while relying upon God's mercy for protection from misfortune is just plain irresponsible, and

---

15. Babylonian Talmud, Kiddushin 39b.
16. Babylonian Talmud, Shabbat 129b (also see Yevamot 72a).

it is not appropriate for a person to call upon God to preserve him from calamity under such circumstances.[17]

Nevertheless, it is universally recognized that life is fraught with danger. Crossing the street, riding in an automobile, flying in a plane – all these activites involve potential danger. It is, of course, inconceivable that people be required to avoid such ordinary activities. Such actions are indeed permissible since "the multitudes are accustomed to it"; that is to say, since the potential risks associated with these activities are considered to be acceptable risks by society at large, and those who engage in them are considered to be displaying normative behavior, individuals are granted dispensation to rely upon God, Who "protects the unwary." The person who ignores the risk is allowed to do so, relying upon an extra measure of divine protection.

In a society in which individuals routinely cross streets, drive automobiles, and fly in airplanes, anyone may do so, despite the risks, of course taking customary precautions. The implication of the counter-text is that when a person is engaged in an activity that carries within it a certain degree of socially acceptable danger, he can rely on the proverbial promise, "The Lord protects the unwary." Unlike the text about the "rickety ladder," which taught that one cannot rely on a miracle when there is risk involved, even when one is engaged in the performance of a divine commandment, this counter-text teaches that despite the fact that there is risk or inherent danger, one is permitted to engage in the activity and rely upon God's protection. However, this should not be understood as a promise of God's protection in all such cases.

What happens then, according to the counter-text, if the person does suffer injury as a result of taking the permitted risk? We must remember – this text does not promise that the person will be protected. It only provides an allowance for the individual to engage in the activity. There is no doubt that while engaged in driving a car or even crossing the street, the person who was relying on God's protection for permission to do so could very well become a victim of the potential peril. The counter-text makes no

---

17. The story that follows in the Talmud (Kiddushin 39b–40a) seems to contradict this one, telling the story of Rabbi Chanina who was once tempted to commit a sin of immorality, and resisting, he ran to hide in a bathhouse known to be dangerous. The Talmud concluded that he was protected by the fact that he had resisted the temptation. The placing of this story directly after the story of the death of the dutiful youth further indicates the inconclusive position of the sages on these issues.

promises of divine intervention; it only serves to give permission to take the risk in the first place.

Perhaps the two texts, the two traditions, are not actually conflicting.

According to both texts, there are things that happen in our lives that God does not expressly decree. There are situations that are fraught with danger. If the danger is the kind that society deems to be reasonable, then one is permitted to act, albeit with knowledge that the danger is real, and that if something bad does happen, one cannot put the blame on God. One may be allowed to take risks, but in doing so, one cannot expect a miracle to happen. Such a person takes his life into his own hands. Even one who is engaged in the performance of a divine commandment, who is doing God's bidding, is nonetheless susceptible to the consequences of the "rickety ladders" of life.

Essentially, this tradition opens up unlimited possibilities for explaining tragic events.

For instance, let's return to the restaurant in Tel Aviv. The couple in the neighboring store saw their survival as a miracle. It may very well have been the case. But what does that say about the deaths of the eleven victims of the second bombing there, not to mention the seriously wounded? One approach, the approach of Rabbi Chanina ben Dosa,[18] would be to assume that for some reason, they were not deserving of divine protection.[19] Their death indicated that they had in some way sinned, and such was their resulting punishment. This might have been the case; however, it is not the only possible understanding provided by our tradition.

In a region where suicide bombings are unpredictable and can strike at any time or place, one might extrapolate that we who live here are, at all times, climbing on one very large, rickety ladder. And even more: even with multiple precautions being taken at all times to keep the public safe, it might be argued that when it comes to terrorism, many places in the world can be classified as "rickety ladders." American film star Will Smith, during a visit to Israel together with his wife in April of 2006, was asked if he was afraid to visit Israel at that time. He replied that he was not. "Terrorism happens world over," he said.

---

18. Babylonian Talmud, Berachot 33a, cited in chapter 2.
19. This seems to also be the approach of Rambam in *Guide for the Perplexed* III:17, where he discusses shipwrecks and assumes that both victims and survivors are determined by God's providence.

The World Trade Center, symbol of the power and prestige of the United States, was a "risky" place to work. On February 26, 1993, a car bomb was planted in the Tower One underground garage of the World Trade Center complex. It was placed there by al-Qaida, the same Islamist terrorist group that carried out the September 11, 2001, attacks. In 1993, six were killed, over one thousand injured, and the World Trade Center became identified as a high-profile target for terrorism.

When the *shwarma* stand at the entrance of the old Tel Aviv central bus station was bombed in February of 2006, it was identified then as a clear target for terrorism. Although there are those who like to believe that "lightning never strikes the same spot twice," that is not the working principle with terrorism. (The sister of the heroic security guard, Binyamin Chafuta, age forty-seven, whose efforts prevented the deaths of many others in the February 2006 attack, said that she had asked Chafuta whether he was scared to perform his job, and he had replied: "Why would a terrorist want to come for a second time to the same place and carry out an attack?!") In fact, the vicinity of the old Tel Aviv bus station was the target of terrorist attacks on at least five occasions between October 2002 and April 2006.

Perhaps we might understand that the victims of terror, wherever terrorism strikes, are casualties of a world that is delicately balancing upon a "rickety ladder." Under such conditions, our tradition teaches us that one cannot count on miracles, and innocent people will inevitably suffer and die. Tradition does not say that miracles do not happen (they very well might happen for some), but the point is that those whose lives are ruined or snuffed out need not comprehend their tragic misfortune as directed by God or a part of His divine plan. They are victims of circumstances in which God does not intervene. Unfortunately, it may very well be the case that in a "rickety," unpredictable world, many tragedies will occur that do not emanate from the hand of the Almighty. We carry on our lives normally, going back to the *shwarma* stands, reliant upon the "Guardian of the unwary"; however, we should not misunderstand the permission we have been granted to take these risks as a guarantee of divine protection.

Automobile Accidents

Traffic accidents can rightly be regarded as the worst category of catastrophes facing the human race. Their high numbers, their severity, and the fact that the bulk of those killed and injured are in the prime of life conspire to make traffic accidents truly terrible.

World Health Organization on Road Safety

Road crashes are the second leading cause of death globally among young people ages 5 to 29 and the third leading cause of death among people ages 30 to 44. Road crashes kill 1.2 million people every year and injure or disable as many as 50 million more.... Without immediate action to improve road safety, it is estimated that road traffic deaths will increase by 80% in low- and middle-income countries by 2020....

The human suffering caused by road crashes is huge – for every victim of a crash, there are family members, friends, and communities who must cope with the physical, psychological and economic consequences of the death, injury or disability of a loved one. Crash survivors and their families must cope with the painful and often long-term consequences of injury, disability and rehabilitation. In many cases, the cost of care, the loss of the primary breadwinner, funeral expenses, or the loss of income due to disability can drive a family into poverty.

The human suffering is in itself a reason to act now, but the economic impact is also significant. In low- and middle-income countries, the cost of road traffic injuries is estimated at US$ 65 billion, exceeding the total amount these countries receive in development assistance. Road traffic injuries cost countries between 1% and 2% of gross national product, amounting to US $518 billion every year.[20]

In the early '90s, at the beginning of the "Oslo" period, a certain Israeli rabbinic leader wrote that it is a well-known fact that on Yom Kippur (the Day of Atonement) God allocates a certain number of deaths for the following year. Now it is also well known that Israel has an incredibly high death rate from automobile accidents. So, the rabbi argued, putting these two facts together, one can only conclude that car accidents are the price of the Oslo peace process. If Israeli society had the dedication to continue its war against the Palestinians, the youth who died in car accidents would have died in war instead (after all, there is that quota), but at least it would have been for a holy cause.

---

20. Excerpted from "*World Health Day: Road Safety Is No Accident*," April 7, 2004; http://www.who.int/mediacentre/news/releases/2004/pr24/en/.

Author Philip Yancey wrote, "I once attended a funeral service for a teenage girl killed in a car accident. Her mother wailed, 'The Lord took her home. He must have had some purpose.... Thank you, Lord.'"[21]

Actually, driving a car is inherently dangerous, but it falls into the category of risks taken by the multitudes, and therefore it is permissible. That being the case, when we drive a car, when we take that risk, we do so with complete impunity; however, the end result may nonetheless be tragic. With halachic permission, we take our lives and the lives of our passengers into our own hands. I may drive a car, but if I get into an accident, I have no reason to blame God.

Therefore, I would argue that in most cases, according to the cited Talmudic texts, automobile accidents do not emanate from God. One need not believe that quotas in heaven are filled by taking the lives of teenage drivers who should have otherwise died in battle.

One need not assume that it is God Who takes the lives of young drivers for some unknown purpose. The Talmud permits taking the risks, but makes no promises as to the outcomes. We need not look for meaning, and we need not assume that God has a hand in such tragic events that result from hazardous, even if permissible, activities. One approach in our tradition teaches us that we may understand such tragedies as the unfortunate results of our permitted engagement in dangerous but routine activities.

For those who still have difficulty accepting this possibility, then take comfort in knowing that you are in good company. Following Rabbi Yehudah HaLevi's delineation of the above four categories under which all phenomena fall, he admits:

> All newly created phenomena must fall under one of the four aforementioned categories, be it Divine or otherwise. But since it is conceivable that all phenomena be of the Divine type, the masses have chosen to attribute all to this category. This is because this perspective strengthens one's faith.[22]

---

21. Philip Yancey, *Where Is God When It Hurts?* (Grand Rapids, MI: Zondervan Publishing House, 1977).
22. *Kuzari*, Essay 5, Principle 10, 20:21.

Fate

What is the Jewish tradition regarding fate? Are there experiences or events in life that have been predetermined for us by powers in nature, and not by the hand of God?

Is there a belief in powers that act upon us that are outside of God's direction?

Are there aspects of our lives that are not the results of our actions, for which neither God nor we should be held responsible?

TEXTS
Some Things Are Determined by the Stars

Rava said: "Length of life, children, and sustenance depend not on merit but rather on planetary influence."[23]

Rabbi Chanina said: "The planetary influence gives wisdom, the planetary influence gives wealth, and Israel stands under planetary influence."[24]

Rava, a great Babylonian sage of the fourth century CE, was of the opinion that although there is divine providence in the world, there are certain things that are not governed by God's dictates, but rather they are dictated by *mazal*, literally "planetary influence."

Talmudic sages even discussed the way in which the specific planetary configuration found in the heavens on the night of a baby's birth was destined to affect the individual later in life. Similarities were expected between two people born under the same star. For example, one sage proposed that a person born on Sunday would be renowned; on Monday, angry; on Tuesday, wealthy and with a strong libido; on Wednesday, intelligent and freethinking; on Thursday, compassionate; on Friday, devout. If born on Shabbat, he was destined to die on a Shabbat, and he would be called a great and holy person.[25]

Rabbi Chanina bar Chama, a third-century sage of the Land of Israel, taught that it was not actually the constellation of the day, but that of the specific hour of his birth that was significant. In fact, Rabbi Chanina was of the opinion that a person is at all times under the influence of the planets and constellations. His entire life is predetermined, and there is no

---

23. Babylonian Talmud, Moed Katan 28a.
24. Babylonian Talmud, Shabbat 156a.
25. Ibid.

changing his fate. He can only choose what type of person he will be, what he will do, and how he will respond to his predetermined lot in life.

Throughout the ages, reports of a birth have often raised hope that the newborn baby had been born *b'mazal tov*, or *b'siman tov*. Even today, news of a birth in a Jewish family is greeted customarily by family and friends with the same Hebrew words, expressing hope that the infant was born with good luck – under a good sign, *siman*, or star, *mazal*. Phrases outlive ideas. While the Talmud uses *mazal* to mean "star" or "constellation," this word has come to mean "luck," and most people who use the term have no idea where the term comes from or how it crept into the Jewish vernacular. (When a Jew today politely wishes another *mazal tov*, he conveys wishes for good health or success, unrelated to the original astrological significance.)

In whatever way we decide to understand these beliefs, one thing is for certain: those who accepted the premise that there exist in the world planetary influences were essentially acknowledging that there are many events in life that are not necessarily prescribed by God. Another factor in the universe, call it *mazal* or call it *siman*, was held responsible for certain outcomes or occurrences.

A story is told about another Babylonian-born sage of the third century CE, Rabbi Elazar ben Pedat, which clearly illustrates this belief.

TEXT
The Importance of Being Born at an Auspicious Hour

Rabbi Elazar ben Pedat was quite poor for most of his life. Once, after sustaining a bloodletting for medical purposes, he had nothing to eat. He took the skin of garlic and put it into his mouth; he became faint and he fell asleep. The rabbis coming to see him noticed that he was crying and laughing in his sleep, and a ray of light was radiating from his forehead. When he awoke, they asked him: "Why did you cry and laugh?" He replied: "Because the Holy One, blessed be He, was sitting by my side, and I asked Him, 'How long will I suffer in this world?' and He replied: "Elazar, my son, would you rather that I should turn back the world to its very beginnings? Perhaps you might then be born at a more auspicious hour.' I replied, 'All that effort, and then you will only suggest that perhaps I will be born at a more auspicious hour?'"[26]

---

26. Babylonian Talmud, Taanit 25a.

The humorous banter between Rabbi Elazar and God as recorded in this tale portrays an understanding that God Himself recognizes the existence of forces outside of His own that hold great sway over the fate of human beings. God's reply to Rabbi Elazar indicates that He is not responsible for Elazar's impoverished life. He did not determine that it be this way, and He cannot change it. For even if He turns back the clock and gives Rabbi Elazar a chance to be born again, at a different time, God admits that He still would not be able to guarantee that Rabbi Elazar would be better off.

The mixture of laughter and tears represents a mixed reaction to his dream. On the one hand, his laughter is an expression of relief that his suffering in life was not a proclamation from above, that he is not being punished for some wrongdoing. On the other hand, his tears are shed at the notion that God can do nothing about his impoverished existence. The combination of relief and depression manifest themselves in Elazar's laughter and tears, and this he shares with his colleagues.

According to the teaching of the Babylonian scholar Rava, as well as the earlier teaching of Rabbi Chanina bar Chama of the Land of Israel, some of the most basic elements of our lives are not determined by God at all, but rather by other influences not subject to God's control. The number of years we live, or perhaps even the quality of our lives, the number of children we have (if we have any at all), and the amount of wealth we accumulate – all of these are outside of God's circle of influence according to these sages. Such a statement by Rava, some argue, does not mean God is completely absent from such matters, but just that He is not the sole influence. In any case, this rabbinically adopted direction of thought chooses to relieve God of ultimate responsibility in terms of some of life's greatest challenges.

The manner in which these external planetary configurations influence the direction of our lives remained a contentious issue among Jews for many centuries. We see that the Talmudic rabbis were divided over the issue, and that while some embraced it, others looked for ways to prove it wrong.

COUNTER-TEXT

Everything Is a Consequence of God's Will

Rabbi Yochanan maintained: "Israel is immune from planetary influence."

> **Rav Yehudah said in Rav's name: How do we know that Israel is immune from planetary influence? Abraham pleaded before the Holy One, blessed be He, "Lord of the Universe, I have looked at my constellation and found that I am not fated to beget a child." "Cease your planet gazing," replied God, "for Israel is free from planetary influence."[27]**

Rabbi Yochanan, one of Rabbi Chanina's close students (they comforted each other in the text we cited in chapter 2), seems to have strongly disagreed with his teacher in this instance. Even if there is such a thing as planetary influence, Rabbi Yochanan maintains that it does not affect the Jewish people. The Talmud brings support for Rabbi Yochanan's opinion, citing the teaching of a sage of that same generation, Rav Yehudah of Babylonia, who cites his teacher Rav (a Babylonian sage who lived several generations before Rava). Basing himself upon an interpretation of God's promise to Abraham, Rav taught that the Jewish people are not in any way under the sway of celestial influences. The Talmudic passage points out that although even Abraham was under the impression that the planets and stars have influence over our lives, God teaches him otherwise. That is to say, God states that the Jewish people are not under planetary influences. The text may actually suggest that such planetary influence does exist – it's just that Israel is not affected by it.

The popularity of this perspective – that there is no fate, that nothing is left up to chance – is well documented throughout the Talmud. When a mishap occurred, whether it entailed physical suffering or only financial loss, the sages would often assume it was an act of providence, and that the victim needed to investigate his activities and look for the divine message.

COUNTER-TEXTS
Examine Your Actions

> **Rav Chisda said: If a man sees that troubles have come upon him, let him examine his conduct.... If he examines and finds nothing [objectionable], let him attribute [his troubles] to the neglect of Torah study.... If he did attribute it [thus], and still did not find [this to be the cause], it is evident that these are chastisements of love, as it is said: "For whom the Lord loves, He chastises" (Proverbs 3:12).[28]**

---

27. Babylonian Talmud, Shabbat 156a.
28. Babylonian Talmud, Berachot 5a. The Talmud is unsure if this passage is attributed

> Once four hundred jars of wine belonging to Rav Huna turned sour.... Scholars went in to visit him and said to him: "The master ought to examine his actions."
>
> He said to them: "Do you suspect me of wrongdoing?"
>
> They replied: "Is the Holy One, blessed be He, suspect of punishing without justice?"
>
> He said to them: "If somebody has heard of anything against me, let him speak out."
>
> They replied: "We have heard that the master does not give his worker his lawful share in the grape vines."
>
> He replied: "Does he leave me any? He steals them all!"
>
> They said to him: "That is exactly as the saying goes: 'If you steal from a thief you also have a taste of it!'"
>
> He said to them: "I commit myself to give him [his fair share in the future]." Some report that thereupon the vinegar became wine again; others that the value of vinegar went up so high that it was sold for the same price as wine.[29]

These counter-texts have introduced an alternative tradition to those cited earlier. Rav Huna lived in the same generation as Rav Yehudah, and Rav Chisda lived a generation later. It seems that they and their colleagues assumed that everything that happens is by God's decree. In addition, suffering must be assumed to be a just and deserved punishment, for to assume otherwise serves to indict God Himself for acting unjustly.

However, Rava, living in the generation after Rav Chisda, suggested a very different perspective. His was a more circumspect approach, an approach that perhaps considered that it is improbable to accept that all of the suffering and misfortune in the world is somehow a part of God's divine plan. While for some this approach might sound heretical, for others, it can be a source of great comfort to believe that not everything that befalls us is so deserved.

In this way, the Talmud introduces two very different approaches to understanding God's role in some very significant aspects of our lives.

If you are uncomfortable with the notion that there exist powers

---

to Rava or Rav Chisda. According to our analysis, it makes more sense to attribute it to Rav Chisda, since Rava is on record as believing in planetary influences (see prior text).

29. Babylonian Talmud, Berachot 5b.

outside of God's jurisdiction that control our destinies, then once again, you are in good company. Many have felt this discomfort. As the Meiri teaches:

> Don't pay attention to the alternative view that says that Jews are in fact controlled by *mazal*. That view is the result of some of the sages becoming confused after they saw the lack of order in the manner of humankind's reward and punishment. This confusion is also manifest in Moed Katan (28a), which states that "Length of life, children, and sustenance depend not on merit but rather on planetary influence." This statement was made only because the author saw someone who was a *tzadik* and great scholar who was unsuccessful in these three areas.... These statements asserting the importance of *mazal* were only made in response to their authors' personal experiences or what they observed with others. Thus these are only exceptions to the general rule, that "Jews are not governed by *mazal*." In other words reward and punishment typically determines what happens to a person and not *mazal*.[30]

This strong objection to these Talmudic teachings betrays the cognitive dissonance created by the implications of Rava's and Rabbi Chanina's teachings. Those who embrace a strong belief in God's close management of our world and every aspect of our lives will find it difficult to accept Rava and Rabbi Chanina's teachings at face value. Instead, assuming that the teachings of both Rava and Rabbi Chanina are the result of desperate attempts to explain senseless suffering and hardship in our world provides a way to get around these challenging statements. However, in doing so we throw into question the validity of Talmudic teachings in general. What other comments are then to be considered the result of "confusion"?

On the other hand, accepting these teachings at face value forces many of us to rethink our assumptions about God's role in our lives – an equally difficult challenge for those who maintain a strong faith in the personal providence of the Almighty in all aspects of our lives.

---

30. Meiri, *Beit HaBechirah*, commentary on Babylonian Talmud, Shabbat 156a.

The Powers of Nature

Can Sorcery Overpower God's Will?

"There is none else beside Him" (Deuteronomy 4:35). Rabbi Chanina said, "Not even sorcery." A woman once attempted to cast a spell over Rabbi Chanina. He said to her, "Try as you will, you will not succeed in your attempts, for it is written: 'There is none else beside Him.'"

Has not, however, Rabbi Yochanan declared: "...Sorcery overrules [the decree of] the heavenly council"?

Rabbi Chanina was in a different category, owing to his abundant merit.

Rabbi Chanina further said: "No man bruises his finger here on earth unless it was so decreed against him in heaven, for it is written: 'The steps of a man are directed by the Lord (Psalms 37:23).'"[31]

The sages taught that there is a wisdom possessed by some that is called *keshafim* – translated as "sorcery" or "magic." In explaining the source of sorcery's power, Rabbi Chaim of Volozhin (the Brisker Rav) explained that God conferred upon humankind control over certain "lower" metaphysical powers, powers that come through the stars and constellations.[32] In their belief system, *kishuf* was a part of divine natural law that human beings could control.

Rabbi Chanina seems to teach that there are no such powers capable of being harnessed by human beings in order to supersede God's will. Rabbi Yochanan, his student, disagrees, citing an alternative tradition in the matter which states that indeed sorcery can overrule the decrees of the Divine.

Resolving the conflicting views, the Talmud suggests that Rabbi Chanina was in a unique category, having amassed such great merits in his lifetime as to have been protected from the powers of sorcery.

This insight then colors our understanding of the next statement made by Rabbi Chanina. Rabbi Chanina states, "No man bruises [even] his finger here on earth unless it was so decreed against him in heaven." It would seem clear that when the Talmud places this statement after the comment

---

31. Babylonian Talmud, Chulin 7b.
32. Rabbi Chaim of Volozhin, *Nefesh HaChaim* 3:12.

regarding Rabbi Chanina's unique status, the Talmud wants us to understand this sweeping statement in that same context. That is to say, if you are in the "righteous" category of a Rabbi Chanina, overflowing with merits, then you will not be susceptible to influences that lie outside of God's will. However, for the rest of us there may be other forces at work; things that happen to us may very well *not* be the result of God's direct decree.

Interesting. It was the very same Rabbi Chanina in the text cited earlier (in the text *Some Things Are Determined by the Stars*, above) who taught that wealth and wisdom *are* under the influence of the planets. And there it was actually Rabbi Yochanan who argued that it wasn't so, that Israel is *not* governed by the stars and constellations.

To answer this seeming contradiction, we need to approach their disagreement in a different way.

The issue over which they are arguing relates to the possibility of a human being's actions superseding the will of God. Accordingly, Rabbi Chanina, who believes fully in unchangeable fate, in predetermination, argues that no human being can interfere in God's plan. No human being can take action that is not willed by God and the celestial powers above us. Even if humankind has been given the ability to harness certain powers of nature, no human being can harness those powers in such a way as to commit an act that will actually counter the will of God. That is simply impossible.

Rabbi Yochanan disagrees. Rabbi Yochanan believes that the will of God can be contravened, but not by other celestial powers. Those powers on their own are subservient to God's will. There is only one power in the universe that can take actions that will radically contravene God's will – and that singular power is the human being. And therefore, when a human being does harness the powers of nature, the impact can then bring about effects that are even contrary to God's will.

Humankind is in partnership with God in this world. It is taught that "a person has freedom of choice and freedom of will, and so he can take the life of one who is not worthy of death."[33] It would seem that this is the essence of Rabbi Yochanan's philosophy, and the basis of his disagreement with his teacher, Rabbi Chanina.

Rabbi Yochanan teaches that human beings can take actions that are not in any way representative of the will of God, while Rabbi Chanina

---

33. Rabbi Chaim Ben-Attar (1696–1743), *Ohr HaChaim*, commentary on Genesis 37:21.

emphatically teaches that this is simply not the case. The Talmud comes to teach us that while Rabbi Chanina was not susceptible to such incidents, the average person may very well be so disposed.

Once again, the Talmud has provided us with a dual perspective of God's role in the events surrounding our lives. Included and recorded in the Talmud are the opinions of those who understand that God is the exclusive source of all that happens to us. We have also read the dissenting opinions of those who argue that many occurrences, including those that seriously impact on our lives, are not directly the result of God's decree. That is to say, some things just happen; we need not look for a divine message. Neither should we indignantly point our finger at God, holding Him responsible for our suffering. Rabbinic tradition has provided us with two opposing positions in this matter, thereby offering us different ways to relate to personal suffering.

For some, it is most comforting to understand all suffering and death as purposeful. It is this belief that strengthens one's faith. Perhaps it comes to bring atonement, to enhance reward in the afterlife. Accepting that the suffering or death is the result of God's decree, for some inexplicable but just purpose, maintains order in an otherwise chaotic world.

For others, comfort will come only in believing that God is often not directly responsible for the suffering we endure. For these people, the idea that certain tragic events can come about as the result of nature, chance, or choice, or because of the many "rickety ladders" that we choose to climb, is what enhances their faith in God. Both approaches are representative of time-honored Jewish approaches to personal suffering.

Chapter 4

DO PEOPLE DIE
BEFORE THEIR TIME?

"His Time to Die"

Death of us Army Pfc. Robert J. Settle, April 19, 2006: Robert Settle, twenty-five, of Owensboro, Kentucky, was killed by a roadside bomb in Taji, Iraq. Settle's furlough was only two weeks away; his five-year-old daughter Chloe had been eagerly awaiting his arrival home. "He's in a better place," said Aaron, Settle's brother. "He's waiting for me. God wouldn't have taken him out of this world if it wasn't his time."[1]

***

Death of Afik Ohayon, June 28, 2004: Four-year-old Afik Zahavi-Ohayon was killed by Kassam rockets, which landed on the street in front of his nursery school in Sderot. The Kassam knocked him and his mother, Ruth, down as they were on their way to his school. At the funeral, Itzhik Ohayon, the bereaved father, sobbed, "I just wanted him to tell me 'Goodnight Abba.'" "It wasn't his time to die," Itzik cried. "I would have gone instead of him."[2]

It Must Have Been His Time to Die

When a young person dies or is killed, we are confronted not only with the pain of the loss, but we are forced to come to terms with an acute case of theodicy. Children bury parents – not the other way around. Dealing with the death of children requires much reconciliation. People will find different ways to cope, to give meaning to such deaths.

---

1. Based on the article "us Casualties," *USA Today*, April 19, 2006; http://www.usatoday. com/news/world/iraq/casualties/2006-05-05-april-06-glimpses_x.htm?csp=34.
2. Based on the article from the *Jerusalem Post*, June 29, 2004; http://info.jpost.com/ C002/Supplements/CasualtiesOfWar/2004_06_28.html.

TEXT
Returning the Deposit

Rabbi Meir was studying in the *beit midrash* one Shabbat afternoon, when his two sons suddenly died.

What did their mother [Beruriah] do? She left the two of them on the bed and pulled a sheet over them. When Shabbat concluded, Rabbi Meir returned from the *beit midrash* and asked, "Where are my two sons?" Beruriah answered, "They went to the *beit midrash*."

"But I looked for them there," said Rabbi Meir, "and did not see them." She gave him a cup of wine and he concluded Shabbat with the recitation of *havdalah*. Again he asked, "Where are my sons?" She answered, "Sometimes they go to someone's house, they will soon return." She gave him to eat, and after he ate she said, "My teacher, I have a question to ask you." "Then ask your question," he said.

"At an earlier time, someone came and left a deposit with me, and now he has come to take it back; should I return it to him or not?" He answered, "Is not one who is holding a deposit obligated to return it to his master?" She said to him, "If this were not your opinion, I would not have been inclined to return it."

She took him by the hand, led him to the bedroom, and brought him close to the bed. She removed the sheet from upon them and he saw the two of them lying there dead on the bed. He began to cry out, "My children! My children! My teachers! My teachers!" [Children biologically, teachers in that they enlightened his eyes through their understandings of Torah.] At that moment, she said to him, "Did you not just say to me that we are obligated to return the deposit to its owner?"

Said Rabbi Chanina: With these words, Rabbi Meir was calmed and comforted.[3]

According to this midrash, parting with children is a matter of returning them to God, Who blessed us with them in the first place, according to a plan that only He can fully understand. Just as this notion provided the

---

3. Midrash Yalkut Shimoni, Proverbs, sec. 964.

first-century sage Rabbi Meir with comfort when faced with his tragic loss, so too has this concept spoken to parents in all generations who suffer the premature loss of a child, providing them with some degree of consolation.

At the height of the second Palestinian Intifada, in 2001, Rabbi Shlomo Aviner of Beit El wrote an article entitled "Does Every Bullet Have an Address?" (I cited this article in the introductory chapter entitled the same.) In his article, Rabbi Aviner emphasized that every death occurs exactly when it is that God has prescribed. If, for instance, a soldier going off to defend the country expresses fear, he should be told:

> "Do not fear, for every bullet has an address, and there exists divine providence." If his time has come, the Angel of Death will find him wherever he is. If his time has not come, the Angel of Death will not seize him under any circumstances.
>
> Since it is a mitzvah to endanger oneself for the sake of going to Israel, building Israel, and fighting for the land, there is nothing to worry about. And if something does happen to a person on the way to doing the will of his Creator, then it is a sign that his end had come, his time was up. It would have happened to him even if he had stayed home, for it makes no difference here or there to the angel of death, he will arrive at any location, or better said, he will cause the person to be in the exact place at the exact time.[4]

Rabbi Aviner further explained that not every death in battle is deserved; that is, a person who dies in battle is not automatically considered to have been guilty and deserving of punishment. However, every death is just – even though we may have no suitable explanation. Nothing is left up to chance; God is directing all things, every aspect of our lives. Accordingly, no one dies before his allotted time.

For many bereaved families, this belief is integral to their ultimate consolation. It enables them to maintain their belief in an all-powerful, all-knowing, benevolent God Who has a purpose in His taking the precious life of their beloved child or sibling. Parting with children is a matter of returning the deposit to its owner.

---

4. *B'ahavah u've'emunah*, publication of Machon Meir, Jerusalem, no. 321 (27 Elul, 5761): 9.

According to this tradition, every human being has a certain span of years, days, hours that he has been allotted to live, and death is merely an indication that his predetermined quantity of time has lapsed. Faith in this interpretation of our reality takes blame away from the specific circumstances and allows the mourner to grieve for the loss, without confusion about the events that surrounded it.

However, the understanding expressed by Rabbi Aviner is by no means the final word on this subject. Already hundreds of years ago, an alternate opinion was expressed by the greatly respected rabbi and scholar Yehudah HaLevi, whose position was introduced in the previous chapter.

COUNTER-TEXT
Three Causes for Death
King David, of blessed memory, cited three different causes for death. He said:[5]

"God will smite him" – this refers to the Divine cause.

"Or his day will come and he will die" – this refers to the natural cause.

"Or he will descend into battle and perish" – this refers to the incidental cause.[6]

According to Rabbi Yehudah HaLevi, none other than David himself taught that not all deaths are the direct result of God's will. When it was told to David that his enemy, King Saul, had been located and was currently fast asleep, an easy target, David gave strict instructions that no one was to assassinate him. Rather, David affirmed that Saul was to die in one of three ways:

1) God will kill him directly, or
2) he will die when it is his day to die
   (a concept to be discussed next in this chapter), or
3) he will be killed in battle.

For David, these are three *different* options. And therefore, death in battle was *not* understood to be the result of God's direct initiative or directive. According to Yehudah HaLevi, David was alluding to this understanding, that aside from death by divine will, death can alternatively be the result

---

5. The three quotations that follow are all taken from the same verse: I Samuel 26:10.
6. *Kuzari*, essay 5, principle 10, 20:27.

of *natural* or *incidental* causes. The death of a soldier in battle is in the category of incidental causes according to HaLevi.

So, Teach Us to Number Our Days...[7]

What does Jewish tradition teach us regarding the number of days we are destined to live? As mentioned above, David's second category of three was the possibility that Saul's "day will come and he will die."

How are we to understand this possibility? Is a person's number of days predetermined? What factors might affect this number, adding time or shortening it?

TEXT
The Righteous Will Be Blessed to Live Longer Lives
For it was taught: "'The number of thy days I will fulfill'[8] refers to the years of the generations [the span of life allotted to every human being at his birth]. If one is worthy, he is allowed to complete the full period; if unworthy, the number is reduced." So said Rabbi Akiva.

But the sages said: "If one is worthy, years are added to one's life; if unworthy, the years of his life are reduced."[9]

Although, according to this text, it would seem that every human being is allotted a certain amount of years from the time of his birth, the question that occupies the focus of the disagreement between Rabbi Akiva and the sages is whether or not the way we choose to live our lives impacts upon that quantity of time each of us has been allotted.

Rabbi Akiva takes a very conservative stance, claiming that the best we can do is live a life that is worthy of being granted the predetermined number of days we have been allotted. If we prove to be unworthy, then the number of our days will be shortened.

According to the rest of the sages, however, it is also in our hands to extend the time we have been allotted in this world. If we are "worthy" our lives are extended, and if not, the number of our days is reduced.

This second perspective suggests that the lifespan we are allotted at birth is only a starting point. It will by necessity change, becoming longer or

7. Psalms, 90:12.
8. Exodus 23:26.
9. Babylonian Talmud, Yevamot 49b–50a.

shorter, depending on the way we live our lives. While according to Rabbi Akiva, the years we are allotted at birth represent a maximal allowance of time, according to the sages, it is merely a starting point.

In either case, this text indicates that our actual length of days is the product of the choices we make in life, our worthiness or lack thereof. Both Rabbi Akiva and the sages seem to agree that, in one way or another, the time we spend upon this earth is calculated and fixed through a mixture of predetermination combined with our lifelong accumulation of reward and punishment. That said, although there might be some flexibility in terms of the ultimate allocation of time we are apportioned, our death marks the expiration of that allocation. We die when God determines that we are meant to die, at the moment when the last grain of sand slips to the bottom of our divinely calibrated individual hourglasses.

However, it often seems that there is no direct relationship between worthiness and length of days. Wrote Ramban,

> The question of the suffering of the righteous still stands, for we do not see the world in its completeness…. Behold, how many righteous ones have been killed while studying their sacred books, or when fasting and praying with great sincerity…and those who have died before reaching the age of twenty [the age when Jewish law first considers a person to be punishable for their sins].[10]

What other factors might need be taken into consideration when looking to explain God's role in taking the lives of the righteous before their time?

COUNTER-TEXT
The Righteous May Be Blessed to Live Shorter Lives

One day, Rabbi Yochanan was going on a journey and saw a man gathering figs; strange as it was, the man was leaving those that were ripe and taking those that were unripe. So Rabbi Yochanan said to him: "Aren't the ripe figs better?"

The man replied: "I need the figs for a journey: the unripe ones will keep, but the ripe ones will not keep."

Said Rabbi Yochanan, "This is the meaning of the verse: 'Behold, He puts no trust in His holy ones' (Job 15:15)."[11]

---

10. Ramban, "Torat HaAdam," in *Kitvei HaRamban*, ed. Haim Chavel (Jerusalem: Mossad HaRav Kook, 1988), 2:282.
11. Babylonian Talmud, Chagigah 5a.

This story provides us with an interesting metaphor. The ripe figs represent the righteous ones. While on the one hand the righteous represent qualitatively the very best of the generation, and by all rights, should be rewarded with health and a lengthening of days as a reward for all that they have done, on the other hand, they are most fragile, most trusting, and most naïve, and so, most vulnerable. In a matter of speaking, they will "not keep" much longer, they are bound to soon spoil if they continue on life's journey. Therefore, while they may have the most to offer, the most to contribute to the enrichment of the lives of others, God takes them from this world before their time, in order to preserve their righteousness.

He cannot "trust" these "holy ones" to preserve their own purity for the lifespan that they deserve to live. If allowed to live out the fullness of their years, their holiness is bound to be compromised. Therefore they are taken away from us – some when very young, others in the prime of their lives – in order to protect them from the disgrace or debasement that lies just around the corner.

> The righteous one perishes, and no man takes it to heart; men of kindness are gathered in with no one understanding that because of the impending evil the righteous one was gathered in.[12]

The early chapters of the Book of Genesis relate the names of the first humans to inhabit the earth. Generations are born; they procreate, live out their lives, and then die. Every patriarch of every generation is recorded to have lived some 800 years or more before their death! However, one particular individual, Enoch, who represented the seventh generation of human existence counting from Adam and Eve, lived only 365 years...and then died.

> And Enoch walked with God, and he was not; for God took him.[13]

And so it is explained by the sages that Enoch maintained a righteous lifestyle amidst a generation of evildoers. God therefore "took him" from this world before his allotted time, bestowing upon him life in the hereafter, in order to protect him from what God saw as his inevitable corruption were he to remain alive on earth any longer.[14]

---

12. Isaiah 57:1.
13. Genesis 4:24.
14. Midrash Hane'elam Zohar Chadash, 20.

This midrash serves to explain the enigma of Enoch's severely curtailed life (365 was a short life in early Genesis terms!), and like the interchange between Rabbi Yochanan and the fig harvester in our previous text, it conveys the same rabbinic approach regarding premature death. It suggests that one way of coping with the untimely deaths of the very righteous, as well as the demise of the young and the innocent, is to accept that they were taken from this world for their own good. In search of explanation for the inexplicable, looking for a way to make sense of the suffering of the innocent, this approach assumes that this principle of spiritual protection must be at work.

In 1968, country singer Loretta Lynn released an album entitled *Who Says God Is Dead?* One of the most powerful songs in that album, entitled "Mama, Why?" depicts a conversation between a mother and son, coping with the untimely death of Daddy. Faced with her son's grief, the mother attempts to explain why God took his father.

> You see son,
> God picks the sweetest, most beautiful flowers that grow
> And he makes them the brightest, shiniest stars that glow.
>
> Now Daddy talked with the Lord every day
> And Daddy and God'll be real close
> So let's just say it seems that God takes
> The ones he loves the most.

Although I realize that Loretta Lynn's song "Mama, Why?" is not a Jewish text, I include it as a popular example of coping with an untimely death by turning it around into a positive, just as the midrash has done.

> My beloved has gone down to his garden, to the beds of spices,
> to pasture his flock in the gardens, and to gather lilies.[15]

The rabbis interpreted this biblical verse as a reference to God's practice of taking away the righteous of the world – *gathering the lilies*.[16] I recall years ago when a couple I knew who had lost their one-year-old child asked to meet with me for some counseling. We set to meet in a week's time. When they arrived in my office, they shared with me how much better they were

---

15. Song of Songs 6:2.
16. Jerusalem Talmud, Berachot 2:8; Genesis Rabbah 52.

feeling. Someone they had encountered during the week had suggested to them that their child was taken by God because God gathers up and picks the sweetest, most beautiful flowers that grow, and plants them in his garden on high. This image had brought them great comfort during these difficult times. It is the message of the midrash.

Enoch's premature demise and its rabbinic interpretation are representative of an approach that has helped many people to cope with their tragic losses. This approach considers the tragic death to have been without a doubt the will of God, and it offers those who mourn consolation in knowing that, in the bigger picture, it was for the best. Premature death is actually indicative of divine protection from uncontrollable circumstances, societal forces that would have undone a life of good works. This divine protection is accorded to the deceased because of his or her great worthiness; it should not to be misunderstood as punishment for sin.

According to this rabbinic approach, even the very righteous may not be able to extend their allotted time in this world. For even if they might be deserving of such privilege, God may yet take them away from their worldly existence with only their very best interests in mind.

TEXT
Death of the Righteous Atones for the Living
Rabbi Gurion, others say Rav Joseph son of Rav Shemaiah, said: When there are righteous ones in the generation, the righteous are seized [by death] for the [sins of the] generation; when there are no righteous in a generation, school-children are seized for the generation.[17]

This text suggests that the untimely death of an individual may not be a reflection on the individual's merit or lack thereof; rather, it suggests that the deaths of those who are quite meritorious, or alternatively those who are the most pure and least sinful, can bring atonement for others, perhaps even for an entire generation.

On March 6, 2008, a man dressed similar to a yeshiva student appeared at the entrance of the Mercaz HaRav Yeshiva in Jerusalem, carrying a "parcel" that concealed a Kalashnikov assault rifle and numerous magazines

---

17. Babylonian Talmud, Shabbat 33b.

of ammunition. He entered the yeshiva and began to fire indiscriminately at the students who were learning in the library. During the pandemonium that followed, scores of screaming students tried to escape the hail of bullets, including jumping out of the yeshiva's second- and third-story windows. In the end, eight students were killed, mostly teenagers ages eighteen and under. Eleven others were wounded, three critically. Some of the victims were found still holding the sacred books from which they were learning before they were murdered.

At the funeral the next day, former chief Rabbi Mordechai Eliyahu was among those who bore the grave task of eulogizing the young victims. Amidst his heartfelt comments, he said, "When there are [heavenly] accusations against the people of Israel, God takes the righteous in order to atone for the sins. They are roses who were picked and thanks to them God will have mercy on us."[18]

How does this work? Do we Jews believe that the death of some can provide atonement for others? As difficult as it may be to grasp, this does represent the traditional understanding of this Talmudic text. The collective is atoned for through the tragic death of one or some of its great ones.

Some sages, uncomfortable with this understanding, explained this Talmudic text and others like it differently. The death of the righteous or the young student brings with it atonement for the entire generation, because it causes people to be moved, to become introspective about their own lives and deeds, to repent for their sins.

A young American yeshiva student studying in Israel at the time of the Mercaz attack reflected this same sentiment when he wrote:

> What was I supposed to take from all of this? What was the message I was supposed to get? What was the lesson I was supposed to learn? That was the question that was driving me crazy. That was the question that I had to ask and answer. It seems to me, that's the question that everyone must ask and answer, each in his or her own way.[19]

---

18. Haaretz online edition, March 10, 2008; http://www.haaretz.com/hasen/spages/962027.html.
19. Noah Jacobson, March 16, 2008. Unpublished quotation.

It Wasn't His Time to Die

As Itzhik Ohayon buried his four-year-old son, Afik, he cried out, "*It wasn't his time to die.*"[20]

Rabbi Shlomo Aviner seemed to suggest that there is no such thing, and many of the sources we have seen thus far in this chapter corroborate that belief. Albeit some texts indicate that one's allotted number of days in this world may be extended or shortened for a variety of reasons, that too is a direct result of God's will.

However, another well-respected contemporary Israeli rabbi offered a very different perspective, specifically as regards cases of soldiers killed in battle, or others who become themselves victims of violence, or casualties of tragic mistakes or negligent mishaps.

On June 11, 1985, a school bus carrying middle-school students to a field trip collided with a train. Nineteen seventh-graders and three adults were killed in the tragic mishap.

Rabbi Hayim David HaLevy, *z"l*, former chief rabbi of Tel Aviv-Jaffa, was called upon to address the question "Is everything God's decree? Are there no incidents of human error in the world that can be considered the cause of accidents like this one?" Rabbi HaLevy responded,

> There certainly are [accidents caused by human error rather than by God's decree].... This way of thinking is far removed from the masses who see in every occurrence without exception the hand of God. This approach has been handed down to us by Arab fatalism, a way of thinking that interprets everything that happens to a person and to humanity as decreed from the beginning, and that there is no escaping or preventing it from happening. Other religions have adopted that way of thinking, and have tied it to the will of God, Who decrees all.
>
> This is not the way of thought of our holy Torah.... When we know for certain the specific cause of a human tragedy, there is no need to search for divine decrees or punishments, for it can categorically be the case that it is the result of chance and carelessness that brought it about....[21]

---

20. *Jerusalem Post*, June 29, 2004; http://info.jpost.com/C002/Supplements/CasualtiesOfWar/2004_06_28.html.
21. Hayim David HaLevy, *Aseh Lecha Rav* (Tel Aviv: Society for the Publication of the Writings of HaRav Hayim David HaLevy, 1986), 7:287–88, question 59.

Rabbi HaLevy based his position on an interpretation of Rambam,[22] as well as the Sefer HaChinuch's analysis of the mitzvah of *ma'akeh*, the biblical commandment to erect a fence upon one's roof:

> "Then you shall make a fence for your roof" (Deuteronomy 22:8); and the meaning is that we are to build a wall about our roofs and about pits, ditches, and their like, so that no being will stumble and fall into them or from them....
>
> At the root of this mitzvah is the fact that even though the Holy One, blessed be He, pays special attention to the details of human beings and knows their deeds; and all that happens to them, good or bad, is by His decree and His ordainment, according to their merit or their guilt...nevertheless, a person needs to guard himself from chance occurrences that are usual in the world. For God created His world and built it on the foundations of the pillars of nature; He decreed that fire should burn, and water should extinguish a blaze. And so likewise nature makes it inevitable that if a huge stone should fall on a person's head, it will crush his brains; or, if a person should fall from the top of a high roof to the ground, he will die....
>
> Now, since God subjugated the body of humankind to nature...He commanded him to guard against mishap. For nature, to whose power he is subject, will wreak havoc upon him if he will not be guarded against it.
>
> In fact, though there are some few humans whom the King delights to honor on account of the immensity of their kindly piety and the devotion of their spirit to His ways...such as the great and holy patriarchs, and many of the descendants who came after them...the great majority of people...being sinful, would not merit to attain this great level. Therefore the Torah commands us to guard our dwellings and our locations so that death should not befall us by our mistakes, and we should not endanger our lives relying on a miracle....[23]

Sefer HaChinuch interpreted the inclusion of the mitzvah of *ma'akeh* in the Torah as proof of the existence of *mikreh*, of chance occurrences in

22. Hilchot Taanit, 1:9.
23. Charles Wengrov, trans., *Sefer HaChinuch* (New York: Feldheim, 1992), 5:195–99, mitzvah 546.

our world. The only explanation for there being a need to take such a precaution, as described by the Torah, is that tragedies can occur that are not God's will, and so therefore it is our responsibility to take preventative measures to avoid them.

Later in 1985, Rabbi HaLevy received a letter from someone who had read of his response to the school bus catastrophe and was looking for further clarification.

> One issue is not clear to me from your essay: in the case of soldiers that fall in war, are their deaths by chance, or is it the case that each soldier who falls is decreed to be killed in that battle?

Rabbi HaLevy answered:

> That which appears to me from the sources is that this is not a natural death that was decreed ahead of time, that is to say, that the time of death was ordained ahead of time for the one who dies in battle. Just the opposite! Any chance occurrence like this or any other is to be considered as a death that has occurred before its proper time, and therefore it is logical to assume that it too is by chance, for if the grenade had fallen several meters away, the soldier would not have been harmed.... One who dies in war did not die at the hands of the Angel of Death, at his proper time, and therefore it would seem logical to conclude that is was by chance, and not by a special decree against specific people.
>
> May Hashem guard the lives of all those who go out to battle and return them home in health and unharmed.[24]

The suggestion that death is not always God's will, that people do not always die according to God's decree or as punishment for sin, seems to be at the root of the following Talmudic story as well.

TEXT
The Death of the Righteous Is Beyond Explanation
It once happened that a certain scholar who had studied a great deal of both written and oral law, and had diligently learned from scholars, died in his prime.

---

24. Hayim David HaLevy, "*She'eilot v'teshuvot ketzarot*" in *Aseh Lecha Rav* (Tel Aviv: Society for the Publication of the Writings of HaRav Hayim David HaLevy, 1986), 7:356–57, question 78.

> **His wife took his *tefillin* and carried them about in the
> synagogues and schoolhouses and complained to the sages,
> "It is written, 'For [Torah] is your life, and the length of your
> days' (Deuteronomy 30:20). My husband, who studied Torah,
> and learned Mishnah, and served scholars diligently, why did
> he die in the prime of his life?"**
> *And no one could answer her.*[25]

The text continues with a visit from the prophet Elijah, who, after inquiring of the widow into aspects of their marital intimacy, declares that the scholar's death was warranted, as he did not thoroughly observe the family purity laws, sleeping in close proximity to his wife at times when this was not halachically permissible. Of course, this very private aspect of their lives is something that no one but God and Elijah could have known.

The postscript to the story has two Talmudic scholars disputing Elijah's claim, offering explanations that come to the defense of the deceased scholar, and once again leaving us without an ironclad explanation for his untimely death.

This story focuses on a woman's attempt to find peace of mind after the tragic death of her young, beloved husband, who seems to have died in the prime of his life. Roaming from scholar to scholar, from house of prayer to house of study, her soul cannot rest until she uncovers an explanation for this inexplicable turn of events in her life.

There are several aspects of this story that I find particularly interesting.

First of all, what do we imagine she was doing, carrying her late husband's *tefillin* from rabbi to rabbi? There is a custom to check from time to time the quality of the script on the parchments enclosed in the *tefillin* boxes. Some actually believe that mistakes or other problems found can be indicative of problems in one's life, or that such inaccuracies might even be the cause of the problems. Perhaps out of desperation she was taking the *tefillin* from one rabbinic expert to another with the hope that they would find something there, in the parchments, to explain her husband's death. Perhaps someone could reveal that it wasn't her husband's guilt that brought about his death, but rather, it was a flaw in his *tefillin* that was responsible for his demise; apparently, one after the other they search to find such an explanation, but none can be found.

---

25. Babylonian Talmud, Shabbat 13a–b. Italics mine.

Interestingly, no one suggests to the bereaved widow a variation on the "Enoch theory." Why is it that no one tries to comfort her by telling her that her righteous husband died exactly for this reason – that he was so very righteous?! Instead of searching his *tefillin* for the answer, why doesn't one of them just assume that since he was a scholar, he was taken in his prime for his own good? No one chose to explain to her that her husband died in the prime of his life in order to protect him from becoming corrupted. Why is this traditional explanation not forthcoming from these sages?

It seems to me that this rabbinic text rejects the whole "death for your own good" premise. Instead, it encourages us to assume the opposite: if this scholar was taken so early in life – a scholar who was ostensibly worthy of living out all of his days and then some – something must not be right. And so, they search the *tefillin* for an answer that is simply not forthcoming. They remain bewildered.

Since the rabbis only knew the man as he presented himself to the public eye, they were not in a position to identify a single flaw in his behavior. It takes the likes of the prophet Elijah, who can see into his private life as well, to uncover the dead man's transgression and to proclaim, "Blessed be the Omnipresent for slaying him, that He did not condone his behavior…."

If the story had stopped there, the moral would have been clear: "Don't look at the container, but rather at what is contained inside."[26] If a righteous scholar dies tragically, as in the case described in our story, you can be sure of one thing: he's not altogether righteous.

However, the story does not end there, and it is the postscript of the story that provides us with some fascinating food for thought.

> When Rav Dimi came, he said, "It was a broad bed."
> In the West [the Land of Israel] they said, Rabbi Yitzchak ben Yosef said, "A divider was set between them."[27]

What moved these sages to take on the likes of the prophet Elijah? Are they disagreeing with him, rejecting his explanation, or is something else going on?

I believe that this postscript to the story is meant to convey one of two possible messages about the story itself.

One possibility is that this postscript provides an important twist to

---

26. Mishnah Avot 4:26.
27. Babylonian Talmud, Shabbat 13b.

the story. You see, the widow was in desperate search for an answer, an explanation, a logical means for dealing with her tragedy. Realizing this, Elijah comes up with a reason. He tells her that in essence, her husband was not 100 percent righteous, and so his death was actually warranted as punishment for his shortcomings. The young widow does not respond to the explanation given; however, we can imagine that although it may have been difficult to hear, at the very least it provided her with the explanation for which she was searching. Rabbis Dimi and Yitzchak come then to teach us that in reality, what Elijah offered as justification for his death was not really the case. It is not that they come to claim that Elijah was mistaken; rather, they come to expose Elijah's words for what they really were.

You see, Elijah had realized that this young widow would not be able to accept an explanation that did anything less than provide a logical, just explanation for her husband's death. To suggest that his life was taken by God to protect him from future corruption or to tell her that he died as a result of human negligence – these explanations would not satisfy her. So instead, Elijah suggested that the young scholar had sinned, and that his death, by the hand of God, was deserved. Elijah told her what she needed to hear: that there is order and reason to everything that happens in the world. The testimonies of the later rabbis as to the actual circumstances of their private life, serving to vindicate the young scholar, are included in the postscript of the story in order to clarify this point.

However, another approach relates to the intentions of the Talmudic editors. By including the responses of these two rabbis as the epilogue to the story, a powerful lesson is being conveyed to us.

Perhaps Elijah's assessment of the situation is the absolute truth. The young sage was sinful and therefore he did not merit divine protection from the natural causes that took his life. It is interesting then that two sages, one from Babylonia and the other from the Land of Israel, both weigh in to contradict Elijah's assessment. Their words are included in order to reject the notion that every death, especially the untimely deaths of the righteous, must be explainable. They wished to declare that despite the fact that Elijah, in this specific case, had entered the story and had proclaimed the reason for the scholar's death to be his negligence in the laws of family purity, looking for explanations for death in such cases is not recommended.

Are we to understand that Rabbi Yitzchak, who traveled from the Land of Israel, showed up in Babylonia and had some sort of insider information?

Unlikely. Instead, I would suggest that upon hearing the story, he chose to reinforce the notion that it is the first part of the story that we are to emulate, not the second part. That is to say, when the first part of the text claims that none of the sages could answer the young widow in her quest for understanding, we are meant to learn from this that none of them considered such conjecture to be appropriate. There is no sufficient human way of "explaining" tragedies such as these. And so, in proper response to her request, they listened attentively, sympathized, but did not dare offer what would amount to incomplete rationalizations, no matter what they would have suggested. Could it possibly be satisfactory to blame his death upon a mistake found in his *tefillin*? Could any proposition, even the suggestion that he was taken by God for his own good, serve to comfort this woman in her grief? No. Only Elijah, with his prophetic credentials, could be so bold as to "explain" the scholar's death. Hearing it from Elijah, she would consider it to be the truth. However, if a fellow human would make such a conjecture, it would not satisfy the sufferer. Rabbis Dimi and Yitzchak drive this point home by claiming that as mortals, we are required to give the benefit of the doubt – we would see that the bed was wide, we would assume that a divider separated them, we would not and should not jump to conclusions. Ours is not to search for explanations or to assume that such tragic deaths are the product of divine justice. Even though the widow expresses her need to know, ours is not to presume that we can ever know, nor to assume that this is what God must have wanted.

"A Time to Be Born, a Time to Die"[28]

There is a general sense in Jewish tradition that when a person's time is up, there is nothing that can be done about it. During the Al-Aqsa Intifada, Israelis dealt with the dangers of day-to-day living in different ways. Drive-by shootings in the West Bank became commonplace. Israeli families living in the West Bank settlements were making difficult life-and-death decisions every time they got into the car to drive to work in Tel Aviv, or to take their children along to attend a family celebration in Jerusalem. Some chose to wear flak jackets every time they got into the car; others did not. In discussing the issue with a couple who had decided that they and their family would more-or-less continue to live their lives as they had always done, they expressed to me the belief that it was all in God's hands,

---

28. Lamentations 3:2.

and that when He decides that your time is up, then your time is up. In fact, Judaism does espouse this tradition as expressed in the context of the following Talmudic tale.

TEXT

No Escaping the Angel of Death

There were two scribes that attended on King Solomon, Elichoreph and Achiyah....

One day, Solomon noticed that the Angel of Death looked sad. Solomon asked him: "Why are you sad?" He replied: "Because they [the heavenly court] have demanded from me the two scribes that dwell here." Solomon had demons take them to the city of Luz [a legendary city where no one dies]. However, as soon as they reached the gates of Luz, they died. The next day, Solomon noticed that the Angel of Death was happy. He asked him: "Why are you so happy?" He replied: "Because you sent them to the very place where they were supposed to die." Solomon thereupon uttered the saying, "A man's feet are responsible for him; they lead him to the place where he is wanted."[29]

As this Talmudic text indicates, even the wisest of men, King Solomon himself, could not impact upon the destiny of his loyal servants in the face of the decree of the Angel of Death. Their time was set, and attempting to alter fate proved to be a fruitless endeavor. As Rabbi Aviner taught, everyone's time is pre-allotted. There is no changing that – at least, no humanly possible way of changing it.

COUNTER-TEXT

Staying the Hand of the Angel of Death

Even the Angel of Death gave Moses something, as it says, "He burned the incense and atoned for the people. And he stood between the dead and the living, and the plague was restrained."[30] If the Angel of Death did not give this secret to Moses, then how did he know to do it?[31]

---

29. Babylonian Talmud, Sukkah 53a.
30. Numbers 17:12.
31. Babylonian Talmud, Shabbat 89a.

When Moses and the people of Israel faced rebellion from Korah and his followers during their wanderings in the desert, their actions led God to cast a plague upon the people. A total of some fifteen thousand people died as a result of that punishment. At one point, it looked like the plague was uncontrollable, and all would soon be lost. Suddenly, without divine instruction, Moses directs his brother Aaron to take incense and burn it amid the people, standing between the dead and the living. There is no explanation in the Torah text itself as to how Moses knew to do that. Assuming that he must have learned it from somewhere, the Talmud suggests that he learned this "trick" from the Angel of Death himself.

The implication of this story is that contrary to the lesson derived by King Solomon in the previous text, there is at least one way to stay the hand of the Angel of Death, and Moses was privy to that information. The rabbis are thus intimating that it is actually never too late. Even if the Angel of Death has been sent to terminate life, he can be stopped; it is not a done deal in any way. Although our text conjectures that Moses must have been taught this secret from the Angel of Death himself, it clearly implies that there are ways to escape death's grasp. We are meant to understand that those people who survived the terrible plague survived not based on special individual merit, nor because it just wasn't their time. They survived because Aaron took action according to Moses' instructions. If Aaron had not taken action, then many more would have died – not because it was ordained that their time was up, but simply because the plague would have devoured their lives.

It seems to me that this short aggadic elucidation on an enigmatic incident in the Torah is much more than this; it seems to me that in this suggested solution to the dilemma in the text, the rabbis are acknowledging that an individual's time of death is not fixed in stone. The human decisions that are made in a given set of circumstances have the power to determine whether death will come about or be postponed.

This text may very well serve to reinforce the position that Rabbi HaLevy advocated. Commanding a specific maneuver at a specific moment may very well save the lives of many soldiers. Not ordering that maneuver might bring about their deaths. Those whose lives are spared as a result of the maneuver may very well feel grateful to God; however, they should express their gratitude to the commanding officer as well. At that moment, their lives were in his hands, and his decision to "take the hill" was just the right "incense" that was needed at that moment.

A certain policeman decides one day to reroute traffic on a major thoroughfare where there has been an oil spill. His decision may prevent the deaths of many drivers. Would we say that the people that would otherwise have died that day were the beneficiaries of a miracle? Was the policeman sent that day to prevent their deaths? Or, can we say that the policeman, acting like Moses, applied what he knew to do in order to spare the lives of innocent drivers who would have otherwise died that day, not because it was their time, but because they would have been the victim of an accidental oil spill?

Of course, you might want to argue that in both of these cases, as well as the case of Moses and the plague, it was all directed by God. According to this approach, each Israelite in the desert who was saved from the ravages of the plague specifically deserved to be saved, and each of the fifteen thousand who were killed deserved death. And, while it may have been Moses' quick thinking that technically saved their lives, it was in the end God's will that decided at that moment who would live and who would succumb to the plague.

However, the rabbis in this particular Talmudic text didn't choose to go that route when explaining Moses' initiative. Instead, they credit Moses with having secret information that he, on his own initiative, made use of at this critical moment to save thousands of lives. They do not suggest that it was God Who had instructed him to do this.

Again, such an explanation indicates a willingness on the part of the sages to allow for the possibility that human action does play a significant role in determining when, where, and how our lives come to an end.

COUNTER-TEXT
The Angel of Death Is Not Perfect

Rav Joseph, when he came to the [following] verse, wept: "But there are those that are swept away without judgment" (Proverbs 13:23).

Is there anyone who dies before his [allotted] time? – Yes, as in the story [heard] by Rav Bibi ben Abaye, who was frequently visited by the Angel of Death.

[Once] the Angel of Death said to his messenger: "Go, bring me Miriam, the women's hairdresser!" He went and brought him Miriam, the children's caregiver.

He said to him: "I told you Miriam, the women's hairdresser!"

Answered the messenger: "If so, I will take her back."

Said the Angel of Death to his messenger: "Since you have brought her, leave her be. But how were you able to get her?"

"She was holding a shovel in her hand and was heating and raking the oven," said the messenger. "She took it and put it on her foot and burned herself; in this way, I noted that her *mazal* was impaired, and I took her."

Said Rav Bibi ben Abaye to the Angel of Death: "Do you have permission to act in this way [to take the lives of the innocent]?"

He answered him: "Is it not written, 'But there are those that are swept away without judgment' (Proverbs 13:23)?"

Rav Bibi countered: "But behold, it is written: 'One generation dies, and another generation replaces it!' (Ecclesiastes 1:4)."

He replied: "I have charge of them till they have completed the generation, and then I hand them over to Dumah [the messenger]!"

He [then] asked the messenger: "But in the end, what do you do with her years?"

[The messenger] replied: "If there be a rabbinic scholar who overlooks his hurt, I shall give them to him in her stead."[32]

This aggadah is nothing less than alarming. It clearly implies that there are deaths that are not meant to happen. In fact, the simple understanding here is that there are deaths that occur because of a mistaken communication between the Angel of Death and his messenger. Paperwork errors! Further, the text implies that when a mistake is made, there is nothing that can be done about it! The unlived years of the deceased can, at best, be credited to the life of someone else, someone deserving of reward.

What are we to make of this surprising text?

Rabbi Aviner[33] teaches that this text is not that alarming. For, he explains, the mistakes of other beings – be they human or angelic – are actually all part of the plan. In other words, God has willed these mistakes to happen, and their results are representative of God's very plan.

---

32. Babylonian Talmud, Chagigah 4b–5a.
33. Aviner, *B'ahava u've'emunah*, no. 321 (27 Elul, 5761): 9.

"Mikreh" – It Was an Accident

While I can appreciate Rabbi Aviner's need to reinterpret the text, it makes more sense to me to read it in a straightforward fashion. The text comes to reinforce for us that there are people who die without God willing it, as a consequence of the laws of nature, by accident or chance occurrence, as described by the Sefer HaChinuch above. This may not sit well with everyone, but I believe that the text is very clear.

The opinion being voiced here in the form of a story maintains that there are those who die before their time. Rather than necessarily understanding the text super-literally, that these mistaken deaths are the specific result of miscommunication between the Angel of Death and his messenger, I read the text as presenting an opening for consideration. The story is teaching us that it is quite possible for a person to die before his time. The miscommunication that serves as the basis of the mix-up in this Talmudic text is merely a fanciful way of teaching this critical lesson. The Angel of Death thus represents simply the arrival of death, which may come about through error. Just as Miriam "the children's caregiver" died when she was mistaken for another Miriam, so too others may die by mistake. The mistake, however, need not come from the top. That is not the salient message of this story.

People make mistakes that lead to their untimely, premature deaths. While the story places the blame for the mistake squarely on the shoulders of the Angel of Death and his messenger, I believe that the fundamental message of the story is that there are deaths that do come about by mistake in our world. This Miriam seems to have accidentally burned herself, and may have died from severe burns. It was not "her time" to die, but as a result of this tragic mishap, her life came to a premature end.

It is interesting to note in this text that God is completely absent from the story. The Angel of Death occupies the center of the story; it is he who sends along a messenger to do his bidding.

God is nowhere to be found, because He is not to be blamed nor held responsible in such cases. In fact, these sort of deaths are not His will. And, according to the following sages, such accidental deaths are actually quite common.

TEXT

Ninety-nine Percent of Deaths are the Result of Negligence
Rav and the great Rabbi Chiya – both of them said that ninety-

nine die by the eye, and one by the hands of heaven.

Rabbi Chanina and Shmuel – both of them said that ninety-nine die through exposure to cold, and one by the hands of heaven.

Rabbi Shmuel ben Nachman said in the name of Rabbi Yonatan: "Ninety-nine die by heat wave, and one by the hands of heaven."

And the sages said: "Ninety-nine die as a result of negligence, and one by the hands of heaven."[34]

It couldn't be stated more clearly than this. According to these sages, in the vast majority of cases death is neither the result of divine punishment nor divine will of any sort. The "eye" (to be discussed below), cold, heat, and general negligence are the main causes of death. And lest we think that these are just mechanisms for bringing about divine judgment, vehicles through which God enacts His unalterable will, the sages are careful to point out that only *one in every one hundred* deaths are actually brought about through the will of heaven. Those who die of cold or heat or general neglect, and from the illnesses that result from these, have not been sentenced to die by the Almighty. Rather, through their actions or the actions of others, they have brought their deaths upon themselves.

What is the meaning of the "eye"?

The great first-century Torah scholar, Rabbi Yehoshua, identified three character traits that he claims "drive a person from this world."[35] The first of those traits is called an "evil eye." It is explained that Rabbi Yehoshua is referring here to the harmful quality of envy or jealousy, insatiable lust for wealth or power. Envy burns inside you, as you hopelessly long for something you cannot have. This internal inferno affects your soul, as well as your physical being. Jealousy kills, it eats you up from the inside out, and it "drives you from this world."

The story is told that when Alexander the Great died, he stood before the gates of paradise and demanded that he be admitted. However, he was told that only righteous people are welcome. He declared that as a monarch he demanded some sort of compensation. He was then given a human eyeball. This was placed on one side of a scale, while on the other

---

34. Jerusalem Talmud, Shabbat 14:3.
35. Mishnah Avot 2:16.

side was piled gold and silver. The scale tipped to the side with the eye. He then piled more and more gold onto the scale, but still the eye was heavier. Alexander was confused and asked his wise men for understanding. They replied that it was the eyeball of a human being, which is never satisfied. He asked them how they knew it to be so. They took a little dust and covered it, and so the scale immediately balanced.[36]

Rav and his uncle Rabbi Chiya, two third-century Torah scholars, teach us of the high incidence of people who find no satisfaction with their lot in life, always looking for the greener pastures. "Ninety-nine out of one hundred" harbor this envy, referred to as the "eye" or the "evil eye," constantly dwelling upon others' possessions and good fortune, to the extent that it seriously affects their health and ultimately brings about their death.

This text presents a minimalist approach to God's involvement in determining the time and place of our deaths. Our deaths are normally the result of negligence, the way we choose to live our lives, or the environmental conditions that surround us. Death brought about through direct divine intervention is a rarity.

According to some sages, deaths occur as a direct result of God's will. God may take a person because his predetermined allotment of time is up. Alternatively, a person may be taken by God to protect him from corruption that lies ahead, or because God wants to bring him close to Him. Righteous ones may be taken to provide atonement for the generation in which they lived. Additional positive, purposeful suggestions for suffering and death are offered by our sages.

However, another stream of rabbinic thought suggests that certain deaths – in fact according to one tradition, most deaths – occur by *mikreh*, through circumstances that are not in any way representative of God's will. Accidents happen all of the time, and it is not for us to assume that every misfortune, every case of suffering or tragic death, is the manifestation of the divine will. Rather, more often than not these are the results of human negligence or the indiscriminant effects of our surrounding environment.

---

36. Babylonian Talmud, Tamid 32b.

Chapter 5

WHAT IS THE SOURCE OF EVIL
AND SUFFERING IN THE WORLD?

I form light, and create darkness;
I make peace, and create evil;
I am the Lord, Who does all these things.

(Isaiah 45:7)

In our quest to understand the ways of God, His involvement in our lives and in the lives of our fellow inhabitants of the planet, we are often struck with the presence of what we refer to as "evil." How can God allow evil to exist?

The Evil We Experience Is Caused by God

The above verse from Isaiah states quite clearly that not only does God allow for evil, but that God is the source, the creator of evil, the maker of calamity. To encounter the dark side of the world, the destructive force of nature, or the sinister side of humanity, is to meet up with a form of God's plan.

TEXT
Destruction Is Directed by God
Rabbi Abba ben Kahane said: Never does a serpent bite unless directed to do so from above, and neither does a lion tear apart unless directed to do so from above, and neither does a kingdom attack others unless directed to do so from above.[1]

According to Rabbi Abba, a third-century scholar of the Land of Israel, calamities are all initiated by God, whether they be the destructive forces

---

1. Ecclesiastes Rabbah 10:12.

of nature or the violent actions of humankind. They have been sent through the will of God, wreaking havoc upon the world, inflicting pain and suffering, producing orphans and widows alike. Assuming that God does not impose pain without reason, we are to conclude that all such suffering is warranted; it is meaningful and purposeful.

This approach to evil and suffering serves for many as the basis for seeking meaning and understanding when faced with personal or national catastrophe. This model assumes that no suffering is without meaning and that it is appropriate to search for explanations, to ask the question: *Why did God do this?*

For example, Rabbi Joel Teitelbaum, the Satmar Rebbe, wrote these words following the victory of the 1967 Six-Day War:

> However, it is clear as day to anyone who can perceive truth that the source of all suffering, including the dangers of war, is the outcome of the existence of that Zionist state, that is of no value or benefit either to God or to the Jewish people. On the contrary, that state is the cause of all suffering and destruction, [responsible for the] uprooting of religion and the Torah. The Zionist government is the one who ignited the anger of the Arabs by provoking them in various ways, and were it not for the stubbornness of these wicked rulers there would not be the danger of war. Even now, if they were to give up their state and government, they would doubtless remove the anger of God from the Jewish people, and these dangers and deaths would not befall the Jewish people.[2]

Seeking the Hand of God amid Natural Disaster

The December 26, 2004, Indian Ocean earthquake, which had a magnitude of 9.3, triggered a series of lethal tsunamis, one of which killed approximately 230,000 people (including 168,000 in Indonesia alone). This made it the deadliest tsunami in recorded history, as well as one of the largest earthquakes and worst natural disasters ever. The tsunami killed people over an area ranging from the immediate vicinity of the quake in Indonesia, Thailand, and the northwestern coast of Malaysia, to thousands of miles

---

2.   Rabbi Joel Teitelbaum, *Al hageulah ve'al hatemurah* (Brooklyn, NY: Jerusalem Publishers, 1981), 85–86.

away in Bangladesh, India, Sri Lanka, the Maldives, and even as far as Somalia, Kenya, and Tanzania in eastern Africa.

Hurricane Katrina was one of the deadliest hurricanes in the history of the United States. It was the sixth-strongest Atlantic hurricane ever recorded and the third-strongest land-falling US hurricane on record. Katrina formed in late August 2005 and caused devastation along much of the north-central Gulf Coast of the United States. Due to its sheer size, Katrina devastated the Gulf Coast as far as one hundred miles from the storm's center, having catastrophic effects on the city of New Orleans, Louisiana. More than eighteen hundred people lost their lives in Hurricane Katrina and in the subsequent floods, and some two hundred thousand families were displaced from their homes.

Faced with tragedies of this magnitude, those committed to the search for understanding and meaning reflected on the possible divine messages that should be associated with these catastrophes.

For many who will read the following collection of commentaries and opinions, these ideas will not sit comfortably. However, for people who believe that suffering and destruction, like everything else in our world, is a product of God's will, the search for meaning is completely consistent with faith in God. In fact, to avoid doing so is to discount the significance of the major historical event, to deny the powerful hand of God in our world, to ignore the warnings and so risk further devastation.

Divining a Reason for Devastation

In Israel, Sephardic Chief Rabbi Shlomo Amar, one of the country's top religious leaders, called the tsunami disaster "an expression of God's wrath with the world. The world is being punished for wrongdoing – be it people's needless hatred of each other, lack of charity, [or] moral turpitude."[3]

Is Katrina Divine Retribution?

Rabbi Ovadia Yosef, the leading Israeli spiritual mentor of Sephardic Jewry, told an audience in Jerusalem that Hurricane Katrina was United States President George Bush's punishment for supporting the pullout from Gaza and northern Samaria. "He [Bush] brought about the expulsion [from Gaza], now he has his

3. *Washington Post*, January 8, 2005.

own expulsion," said Yosef. "There was a tsunami and there were horrible natural disasters. It's all a result of too little Torah study. Where there is Torah, the world has sustenance…. Hundreds of thousands are homeless, tens of thousands are dead. All that because there is no God there."

…Repent America, an evangelical Christian organization, claimed God brought Katrina to New Orleans to prevent Southern Decadence, an annual event during which thousands of homosexuals openly celebrate their sexuality. Repent America's director, Michael Marcavage, suggested that "this act of God destroyed a wicked city. New Orleans was a city that opened its doors wide open to the public celebration of sin. May it never be the same. We must not forget that the citizens of New Orleans tolerated and welcomed the wickedness in their city for so long."

In contrast, the Iraqi faction of al-Qaida headed by Abu Musab al-Zarqawi praised the coming of Katrina for being "the start of the collapse" of the US, according to the Kuwaiti paper *al-Bawaba.* "Congratulations to the Islamic nation, to our sheikh Osama bin Laden and to sheikh Ayman Zawahiri [bin Laden's deputy] for the destruction of America, which is at the forefront of evil. It is the start of its collapse." According to them, Katrina was sent by God to torment the American empire.[4]

Katrina's "Message" to Jews

Even as much of New Orleans was still submerged, dead bodies floating on the putrid city-turned-lake, live ones waving from rooftops, the accusations flew fast and furious. The loss of life and property during the Gulf Coast destruction was the fault of… President Bush…Louisiana officials…city planners…those who established a city where disaster was inevitable…those who chose to live there…racism…the Department of Homeland Security… FEMA. Choose your villain, or combination of rogues, and point fingers accordingly.

---

4. Matthew Wagner, *Jerusalem Post*, September 8, 2005. Reprinted with the permission of the *Jerusalem Post* and www.jpost.com.

As it happens there is a Jewish concept, too, of finger-pointing at times of catastrophe. But it is of a decidedly different sort. Jewish tradition counsels Jews to point their fingers at themselves.

Katrina devastated the Gulf Coast just before the arrival of the Jewish month of Elul, when observant Jews begin a period of particularly intense soul-searching that reaches its crescendo a month later, on the "Days of Judgment," Rosh Hashana and Yom Kippur. It might seem a bit proud or particularistic, but the belief that God mandated a special mission for the Jewish people carries with it a responsibility not only to strive to live exemplary lives in service to the divine, but also to see world events as messages. While Judaism considers all of humanity to possess potential holiness, and while its prophetic tradition foretells the eventual movement of all of the world's inhabitants to service of God, it also casts the Jews as chosen. And so Jewishly-conscious Jews have always sought to plumb larger events for more personal meaning.

...Although the destruction wrought by Katrina affected a broad swath of the Gulf Coast, the city with which the hurricane has become inextricably coupled is New Orleans. Might the venue of the recent tragedy hold some meaning for us? What occurs, at least to me, is that the "Big Easy" received its nickname from the lifestyle it exemplified, one of leisure and (in the word's most literal sense) carelessness. The city is probably best known – or was, at least until now – for the unbridled partying and debauchery that yearly characterized its annual Mardi Gras celebrations.

I cannot and do not claim to know "why" the hurricane took the terrible toll it did; but our inability to understand should not preclude us – those of us who believe in a God Who wants us to reflect on, and grow from, events around us – from trying to respond to the wind-driven wake-up call by asking a "what": What can I do spiritually as a result? And one message we might well choose to perceive is the need to recognize how belittling to meaningful life is the contemporary culture of recreation and entertainment.[5]

---

5.   Avi Shafran, *Jerusalem Post*, September 13, 2005. Reprinted by permission of the author

Kabbalist Warns of Future Worldwide Tragedies

Rabbi Yitzchak Kaduri, a leading Israeli Kabbalist, called upon Jewry worldwide to return to Israel to save themselves from natural disasters. According to Kaduri, in the future God will send disasters to countries worldwide in order to "sweeten the judgments of the Land of Israel." Says Kaduri, "I am ordering the publication of this declaration as a warning, so that Jews in the countries of the world will be aware of the impending danger and will come to the Land of Israel for the building of the Temple and revelation of our righteous Mashiach (Messiah)."[6]

All of these reports are representative of the same approach to dealing with evil and destruction in our world: looking for ways to give meaning to such catastrophic events, to interpret the divine message that lies within. Saadia Gaon (882–942) believed that everything emanates from God, and therefore it must ultimately be good. Suffering, he suggested, provides us with discipline and points us in the right direction when we might be in danger of straying off the correct path. Suffering is in our best interest. In addition, like others before him Saadia wrote that suffering can serve at times to clear our guilt and provide for greater ultimate reward.[7]

Toward the end of a chapter entitled "Why Does Hashem[8] Bring Suffering," a contemporary author wrote:

To summarize, we have found ten reasons for *yissurim* (sufferings):

- *Yissurim* for personal atonement.
- *Yissurim* which a person brings upon himself.
- *Yissurim* as a warning to get back on course.
- *Yissurim* which cause a person to fully develop his potential.
- *Yissurim* which develop humility in a person.
- *Yissurim* which atone for the generation.

and Am Echad Resources, a division of Agudath Israel of America.

6. Based on the article by Baruch Gordon, "Kabbalist Urges Jews to Israel Ahead of Upcoming Disasters," *Israel National News*, September 21, 2005; http://www.israelnationalnews.com/News/News.aspx/89850.

7. Saadia Gaon, *The Book of Belief and Opinion* (New Haven: Yale University Press, 1948), treatise 5, chap. 3, 213ff.

8. *Hashem* is a traditional Hebrew substitute for using the name of God. It translates literally as "the name."

- *Yissurim* which have a hidden role in *Tikkun Olam*, Rectification of the World.
- *Yissurim shel ahava*, testing a tzadik's faith in order to increase his reward.
- *Gilgulim* (incarnations), suffering in his lifetime to atone for one's deeds in a previous lifetime.
- *Yissurim* which remove temptation, perhaps even requested by one's soul before its descent into this world in order to be spared from repeating sins of an earlier *gilgul*.[9]

In essence, there are two categories of suffering according to this author:

1. The kind that God sends upon you, for your own good.

2. The kind you bring upon yourself.

The first category is the main focus of this author's writing. He has presented nine different subcategories to explain different contexts in which God may want or need to send suffering upon us. Some of the reasons are for one's own personal benefit; others have national or international purposes. Clearly, the author wishes to impart that in most cases, there is meaning in our suffering.

Assuming that is the case, is it our place to interpret such tragedies? Although the midrashic text brought above in the name of Rabbi Abba indicated that all tragedies occur for a purpose, that's where the midrash ends. It does not suggest that the reason is actually discernable, certainly not to those looking on from the sidelines.

There is another slightly different approach to dealing with evil and suffering. One might profess this same belief, that everything that happens is sent by God, but consider it beyond human ability to fathom the ways of God. This approach does not support guessing as to God's purposes when earthquakes strike or hurricanes destroy; however, that's only because it is not our place to interpret, we do not possess the wisdom to know – not because interpretation is necessarily wrong.

Although we know not why God does what He does, there is an explanation. Nothing happens without God decreeing that it should.

---

9. Yaakov Yisrael Baifus, *Longing for the Dawn*, trans. Nachman Bulman (Jerusalem: Feldheim, 1995).

God Does Not Bring Evil Upon Us

We now consider a very different understanding of evil in the world, its cause as well as its meaning. It was alluded to in the second cause listed above, namely, *yissurim* that a person brings upon himself. Known for his rationalist philosophy, Rambam presents his conception of the causes of evil in the following source.

COUNTER-TEXT
We Bring Evil and Destruction upon Ourselves

All the evils that befall man fall under one of three types:

The first type of evil is that which befalls man because of the nature of coming-to-be and passing away, I mean to say because of his being endowed with matter. Because of this, infirmities and paralytic afflictions befall some individuals either in consequence of their original natural disposition, or they supervene because of changes occurring in the elements, such as corruption of the air or a fire from heaven and a landslide....

The evils of the second kind are those that men afflict upon one another, such as tyrannical domination of some men over others. These evils are more numerous than those belonging to the first kind, and the reasons for that are numerous and well known. The evils in question also come from us. However, the wronged man has no device against them.

The evils of the third kind are those that are inflicted upon any individual among us by his own action; this is what happens in the majority of cases, and these evils are much more numerous than those of the second kind. All men lament over evils of this kind; and it is only seldom that you find one who is not guilty of having brought them upon himself. And it is proper to admonish one who has in fact suffered such an experience with the words, "From your hands has this come about"(Malachi 1:9).[10]

According to Rambam, humans experience suffering for one of three reasons, presented in ascending order of frequency:

---

10. Rambam, *Guide for the Perplexed* III:12.

1. We are physical beings, susceptible to the elements.
2. Other humans choose to cause us to suffer.
3. We afflict ourselves through our own choices.

Rabbi Levi ben Gershom (Ralbag, 1288–1344) explained it in this way:

> Now, since it is obvious that God, may He be blessed, is the most
> perfect of all forms, so that there is no comparison between His
> perfection and the perfection of all other forms, it is fitting that
> from God comes only that which is good and perfect to the
> maximum degree possible to that of which He is the form and
> perfection, i.e., all existing things. In general, all evils that occur
> are attributable to matter or to chance. For the causes of evil are
> necessarily in the recipient itself or from some external factor.[11]

Let's consider more deeply these three categories presented by Rambam.

The Elements

Rambam's first category of causes of suffering reminds us that when all is
said and done, we are creatures of the natural world.

> By the sweat of your face you shall eat bread until you are returned
> to the earth from which you were created, for dust you are and
> to dust you shall return.[12]

There is no escaping this harsh truth. As miraculous as we know the human
body to be, so too, it is just as frail and susceptible to the elements; cold,
heat, germs, bacteria, DNA – all of these contribute to a person's well-being
and play a major role in determining both quantity and quality of life.

West Nile Fever: A Rare Epidemic

On September 20, 2000, Israel called the West Nile fever a rare
epidemic. The mosquito-borne disease had by then been the cause
of death for thirteen Israelis. Boaz Lev, deputy director general of
the Israeli health ministry, told public radio that the ministry of
health was not sure what had brought on the outbreak. "It could
be a combination of weather, mosquitoes, birds and chickens."[13]

---

11. Levi ben Gershom, *The Wars of the Lord, Book Two,* trans. Seymour Feldman
    (Philadelphia, New York, Jerusalem: JPS, 1987), 168.
12. Genesis 3:19.
13. Based on the article "Israel-Disease: Israel Declares West Nile Fever an Epidemic,"

Rambam teaches that this is part of the natural way of things, and specific incidents of suffering at the hands of "the elements" should not be interpreted as being ordained by God. Rabbi Jonathan Sacks, a contemporary scholar and rabbinic leader, saw in Rambam's words the "simplest explanation" for natural disaster and catastrophe:

> Natural disasters have no explanation other than that God, by placing us in a physical world, set life within the parameters of the physical. Planets are formed, tectonic plates shift, earthquakes occur, and sometimes – innocent people die. To wish it were otherwise is in essence to wish that we were not physical beings at all. Then we would not know pleasure, desire, achievement, freedom, virtue, creativity, vulnerability and love. We would be angels – God's computers, programmed to sing His praise.[14]

Earth is just that – earthly and imperfect. The nature of the physical is that nothing about it is permanent. Everything physical is bound to change, to shift, to become unstable at one time or another. What we choose to eat, where we choose to live, how we choose to live – all of these factors combine to impact on our lives and how we experience them.

Some scientists suggest that just as human beings do spring cleaning, so too nature cleans out as well. From the microscopic to the mammoth, what we interpret as destruction should actually be understood as part of the process of rejuvenation that the natural world must go through from time to time.

For instance, take hurricanes. Hurricanes down dead tree limbs and even whole trees. This is one way in which nature removes dead trees from the forest, which in turn makes room for more sunlight to shine down upon newer trees. It also dumps large amounts of debris on the forest floor, where bacteria, insects, and worms can decompose these materials and return sorely needed nutrients to the soil. In the wake of a hurricane, there is often a fair amount of flooding and beach erosion. This actually helps to revitalize the beach, move the landscape, and create more homes for the sand crabs, sandpiper birds, and other animals that depend on the beach for their homes and their food.

Agence France-Presse, September 20, 2000; http://www.aegis.com/NEWS/AFP/2000/AF000955.html.

14. Rabbi Jonathan Sacks, "Why Does God Allow Terrible Things to Happen to His People?" *Times* (UK), January 1, 2005.

Now, these events are clearly not so good for human beings with beachfront homes, but it's a fact of nature that our landscape is naturally in constant flux. The earth's crust, for instance, is broken up at earthquake faults and recreated by volcanoes. Over time, mountains rise higher, rivers dry up, and lakes are created and destroyed by flooding.

By the 1940s, ecologists recognized that fire was a primary agent of change in many ecosystems, including the arid, mountainous western United States. In the first sixteen years of Yellowstone Park's natural fire policy (1972–1987), 235 fires were allowed to burn 33,759 acres. Only fifteen of those fires were larger than one hundred acres, and all of the fires were extinguished naturally. When the great Yellowstone Fire of 1988 took place, it was uncontainable, and the result was devastating destruction. Ecosystem wide, about 1.2 million acres were scorched; 793,000 (about 36 percent) of the park's 2,221,800 acres were burned. However, in the several years following 1988, plentiful precipitation combined with the short-term effects of ash and nutrient influx to produce spectacular displays of wildflowers in burned areas. In certain areas of the park where large numbers of a specific species of very tall pine trees burned, their numerous cones dropped to the forest floor. These pinecones require heat to melt resin and release their seeds. In such locations, seed densities ranged from fifty thousand to one million per acre, beginning a new cycle of forest growth under the blackened canopy above.

It is thus acknowledged by ecologists that forest fires help clean out undergrowth and forest floor litter. Lightning is inevitably going to cause fires, and if they are allowed to burn, they usually keep the flammable material to a minimum. Fires also return to the earth its necessary nutrients, which get depleted over years of growing seasons.

And, what about avalanches? Believe it or not, scientists tell us that avalanches are necessary too. The movement of water on our planet is a critical part of natural maintenance. In certain areas, water comes down as snow, freezes for the winter, and then melts back into water come the spring and flows rapidly down from the mountains. In Israel, heavy snows on Mount Hermon bode well for a rise in the water level of the Kinneret, Israel's main supplier of water. When snow seasons begin early, more snow is allowed to accumulate, freeze, and be stored up as ice until the spring thaw. This thaw will then cause widespread flooding. Avalanches are nature's way of removing large amounts of water (as snow) from the higher points and taking them to lower points where they will thaw sooner and reduce the amount of flooding in the spring. They reduce packed ice and thin the snow, making it easier for animals to survive in the snowy regions.

In sum, the destructive forces of the natural world are all for the greater good of the earth and its environment.[15]

Although Rabbi Jonathan Sacks suggests that in the course of a natural disaster Rambam would admit that "innocent people die," a careful reading of Rambam seriously challenges this conclusion. Several chapters later in his *Guide for the Perplexed*, Rambam specifically addressed the issue of victims of natural disasters. While on the one hand he acknowledges that a disaster could be the result of chance – that is, not specifically the will of God – nonetheless, Rambam is unwilling to extend the chance nature of the event to the specific victims as well:

> It may be by mere chance that a ship goes down with all her contents…or the roof of a house falls upon those within; but it is not due to chance, according to our view, that in the one instance the men went into the ship, or remained in the house in the other instance: it is due to the will of God, and is in accordance with the justice of His judgments, the method of which our mind is incapable of understanding.[16]

According to Rambam, a shipwreck itself can be the result of mere chance; however, extending the chance nature of such a disaster to the specific victims as well is not suitable. Who lives and who dies is the direct consequence of God's will.

Why should it be this way? If Rambam could accept that the shipwreck was by chance, why is that he could not see the victims as unwitting casualties of this tragic disaster? And if God is already taking the initiative to determine the victims and the survivors, why is He hands-off when it comes to the disaster itself? If He is ready to direct human choices, to keep certain individuals off the ship and to make sure that others board, then why is He not ready to direct the captain on a course that will avoid the

---

15. The above argument is based in part on the article by Teresa Bondora, "Destruction: Lessons from Natural Disasters," *Home Educator's Family Times*, November/December 2004; http://www.homeeducator.com/FamilyTimes/articles/12-6article10.htm.
16. Rambam, *Guide for the Perplexed* III:17.

storm altogether? In addition, Rambam readily accepts in the next two categories that there are innocent victims of aggression and violence, as well as guiltless victims of bad decisions or unhealthy lifestyles. Why couldn't Rambam consider the victims of a shipwreck as innocents as well?

This strange duality in Rambam has been noted, and some have searched for ways to resolve this seeming inconsistency.[17] It is interesting to consider to what extent Rambam's opinion in this specific matter may have been influenced by a personal tragic event in his own family. In 1173, his brother David died in a shipwreck on the Indian Ocean. His brother was a jeweler and had supported Rambam in his learning. When David died, the family fortune sank with him, and Rambam was forced to practice medicine in order to support himself. Perhaps it was for this reason that although Rambam was willing to acknowledge that the storm at sea and the boat's unfortunate proximity to the storm were a matter of chance, he could not acknowledge that his own brother's death and the subsequent consequences of that death were meaningless. On a personal level, for Rambam, that tragedy had to have come about through the hand of God. Perhaps that is what Rambam was feeling when he wrote that "our mind is incapable of understanding" the justice of God's judgments.

The Choices of Others

The second most-frequent cause of suffering or death, according to Rambam, is related to the choices that others make. We are often outright victims of tragic decisions made by others. At times these decisions are maliciously motivated; at other times, they are the result of split-second decisions in which the perpetrator has no intention to cause harm. While Rambam here offers "tyrannical domination" as his example of this category of suffering, we are all too well acquainted with the tyranny of wild, irresponsible drivers on our roads. Death and suffering as a result of automobile accidents are often brought about through the irresponsible choices of others.

---

17. Rambam himself is aware of this dilemma, and in a later chapter of his book *Guide for the Perplexed* (51), he offers an original idea acknowledging that at times innocent victims do suffer undeservingly. (See chapter 7 of this book for a discussion of that source.) Additionally, in his introduction to the *Guide*, Rambam indicates that at times his words will appear inconsistent, as a result of the way he chose to compose the book, and that such contradictions will be resolved in subsequent sections of the work.

One Killed, Seven Others Hurt in Traffic Accident near Tiberias

One person was killed and seven others injured Friday in a traffic accident involving a truck and two cars near Tiberias.

Four of the injured are listed as being in serious condition, one man's condition is moderate, and the other two were lightly hurt.

A Magen David Adom emergency medical team evacuated all seven of the injured to Poriya Hospital in Tiberias, although four of them, including a six-year-old girl, were later transferred to Rambam Medical Center in Haifa.

An initial Traffic Police inquiry revealed that the truck was traveling northbound and following a private car, and apparently struck the vehicle after its driver slowed due to a parked car. The driver, a woman, was lightly hurt.

In an attempt to avoid the collision, the driver of the truck swerved into the adjacent lane and hit an oncoming car. The 45-year-old driver of the car was killed, and five of its passengers injured, four of them seriously and one moderately.

The driver of the truck was lightly hurt.

The accident occurred on a narrow two-lane road, with extremely narrow shoulders. Several months ago, five people were killed in a car accident at a nearby section of the road.

Nonetheless, Traffic Police Chief Superintendent Nabil Isawi said the road is well built. "The reason for these accidents is wild driving," said Isawi. "There is no justification for such an accident. If the driver [of the truck] had kept his distance, there wouldn't have been an accident."[18]

Consider this. Over nine million people die worldwide each year because of hunger and malnutrition – five million of which are children. Approximately 1.2 billion people suffer from hunger (deficiency of calories and protein). Yet, at the same time, 1.2 billion suffer from obesity (excess of fats and salt, often accompanied by deficiency of vitamins and minerals). In the United Kingdom, approximately US$38 billion worth of food is thrown away every

---

18. Eli Ashkenazi, "One Killed, Seven Others Hurt in Traffic Accident Near Tiberias," *Haaretz*, January 19, 2007; http://www.haaretz.com/hasen/spages/815572.html. ©*Haaretz* 2007, reprinted by permission.

year, and in the United States, 40–50 percent of all food ready for harvest never gets eaten.[19]

In a world of plenty, a huge number go hungry. And whose fault is this? Clearly Rambam would place the blame squarely upon our shoulders. As Rambam writes, these evils come from us. And what's worse is that "the wronged man has no device against them." They are the result of human choices, where the choices of one human being can destroy the life or the lives of many others. These sufferings too, according to Rambam, do not represent the will of God.

Our Own Choices

The third category suggested by Rambam is the category of evils that we bring upon ourselves. And, teaches Rambam, "these are more numerous" than the others, and we are often in denial as to our direct or indirect fault in the matter.

Heart disease, for instance, is considered the number-one killer in the United States. Twice as many people die of heart disease than of cancer every year in America. High cholesterol, high blood pressure, obesity, diabetes, physical inactivity, tobacco, and secondhand smoke are also risk factors associated with heart disease. Most of these factors are brought about through the lifestyle we choose for ourselves.

Lung cancer is the leading cause of cancer deaths in both women and men in the United States and throughout the world. Lung cancer is the number one cause of cancer deaths in men and has surpassed breast cancer as the leading cause of cancer deaths in women. In the United States in 2004, 160,440 people were projected to die from lung cancer, compared with a projected 127,210 deaths from colorectal, breast, and prostate cancer combined. Only about 14 percent of all people who develop lung cancer survive for five years. About 85 percent of lung cancers occur in a smoker or former smoker. The risk of developing lung cancer is related to the number of cigarettes smoked, the age at which a person started smoking, and how long a person has smoked (or had smoked before quitting).[20] All of these factors are related to our own choices. As Rambam indicates, the horrible suffering experienced by most victims of lung cancer and many victims of heart disease is not to be blamed on God.

---

19. "World Hunger and Poverty," http://www.globalissues.org/TradeRelated/Poverty/Hunger/Causes.asp.

20. "Lung Cancer," http://www.emedicinehealth.com/lung_cancer/article_em.htm.

What Do We Mean by "Acts of God"?

Insurance policies often cite "acts of God" as the conventional description of deaths, injuries, and economic losses arising from floods, droughts, earthquakes, storms, volcano eruptions, landslides, etc. An "act of God" is so extraordinary and devoid of human agency that reasonable care would not avoid the consequences. Accidents caused by tornadoes, perils of the sea, extraordinary floods, colossal fires ignited by lightening, and severe ice storms are usually considered acts of God.

The impression left by this terminology is that God is responsible not only for the natural calamity, but for the ensuing damages caused by the catastrophic event.

TEXT

God's Anger Causes Earthquakes

One verse says, "The eyes of the Lord your God are always looking after the earth, from the beginning of the year until the end of the year" (Deuteronomy 11:12). And another verse says, "Who looks upon the earth, and it trembles, who touches mountains and they smoke" (Psalms 104:32). How is it possible for both of these verses to be correct? At a time when Israel follows the will of God, and tithes appropriately, then is fulfilled the verse, "The eyes of the Lord your God are always looking after the earth, from the beginning of the year until the end of the year," and it does not suffer any sort of damage. However, at a time when Israel does not follow God's will, and they don't tithe appropriately, then is fulfilled the verse, "Who looks upon the earth, and it trembles. He looks upon the earth and it quakes."[21]

According to the tradition described herein, belief in God's providence, in His concern and care for His world and His creations, is seriously challenged when the "mountains smoke" and the "earth trembles," particularly when such natural phenomena bring in their wake death and destruction. While on the one hand we have faith that God is watching over us, that His watchful eyes are upon us at all times, on the other hand we are forced to encounter natural disasters of such magnitude that we may be tempted to reconsider the terms of this belief.

However, this text comes to teach us that we have no reason to doubt God's providence in our world when faced with catastrophic events. In such cases, God is displaying his anger with us, casting destruction and

---

21. Jerusalem Talmud, Berachot 9:2.

devastation upon us through the vehicle of natural disaster in order to rebuke us for our wayward behavior. The commandment of tithing is highlighted here in terms of doing the will of God in general, for it relates directly to our appreciation of the blessings God has provided us via the land. If we don't pay tribute to God and demonstrate recognition of Him as the source of this good, then the land will tremble; that is so say, it will turn from being a source of life and sustenance into a source of death and annihilation.

COUNTER-TEXT
God's Sadness Causes Earthquakes

When the Holy One, blessed be He, is reminded of the great pain of His children suffering under the heels of their Gentile oppressors, He sheds two tears into the Mediterranean Sea whose sound is heard from one end of the world to the other. That is what we call an earthquake." [22]

The message conveyed in this counter-text seems to be very different from the text above. Here, an earthquake is not the punishment or rebuke of an angry God, but rather a by-product of God's sadness and His sympathy for us. In other words, according to this source, when human beings oppress and persecute other human beings, God, so to say, grieves for their suffering. The seismic vibrations felt "from one end of the world to the other" are the result of the "tears" God sheds at the thought of this suffering.

Since we know that God has no tears per se, let me suggest an interpretation of the deeper meaning of this text.

It seems to me that the text purposefully links the imperfections of humankind with the imperfections of the earth to teach an important lesson. In this text, God is described as thinking about the suffering that His nation has endured through the persecutions wrought by other nations. This text seems to clearly articulate that these human atrocities are not God's doing. They have been executed against God's will, causing Him to grieve and even "cry" at the very thought of his creations choosing to be so evil to one another. And, just as the sufferings for which God mourns here are not intentionally brought about by God, so too, natural disasters, such as earthquakes, are not intentionally served up by God. They too come about without divine intent. Like tears rolling down one's cheeks, neither the tears nor the exact place they land are the result of premeditated decisions. Although God

22. Babylonian Talmud, Berachot 59a.

originally created all aspects of the natural world, neither their timing nor the devastation they wreak upon us has been sent upon us by God.

Living in Harm's Way

The scientific origin and the character of many natural phenomena, often referred to as "acts of God," are well understood by now. However, the disaster associated with them often arises as a result of our failure to cope with these phenomena.

The expression "acts of God" implies that we can do nothing about them. However, researchers indicate that this is not exactly the case. Flooding, drought, and famine are caused more often by environmental and resource mismanagement than by too much or too little rainfall. For instance, we humans can make land prone to flooding by removing the trees and other vegetation that absorb this water. We can make land more drought-prone by removing the vegetation and soil systems that absorb and store water. The Ethiopian famines of the 1980s were due to mismanagement, not drought. Israel, a food-exporting country, has a lower rainfall than Ethiopia, but Ethiopia employs little irrigation and its overgrazing and deforestation policies have resulted in a loss of topsoil.

In other disasters such as cyclones and tsunamis, we have often increased our vulnerability by destroying bits of the natural environment that may act as buffers to these extreme natural forces. Such acts include destroying reefs, cutting mangrove forests, and clearing inland forests.

Calling these disasters "acts of God" implies helplessness and inevitability, and discourages a search for ways of preventing or at least minimizing such disasters.

Professor Cyril Domb, emeritus professor of physics at Bar Ilan University and director of the Nebenzahl Institute for Human Safety and Accident Prevention, delivered a lecture in 1995 in which he pointed out that this thesis can be borne out in the following statistics:

> In October 1993 an earthquake of magnitude 6.5 on the Richter scale struck a village in India and claimed 10,000 fatalities. A year later a more severe earthquake struck in California; the papers were full of stories of harrowing experiences, of people trapped in elevators whose shafts were totally distorted etc., but the number killed was less than a hundred.[23]

---

23. Lecture delivered to the Israel Physical Society at its annual meeting in Bar Ilan

Rambam, in the text quoted earlier, indicated that the third category of suffering is the suffering we bring upon ourselves by our own choices. Might the devastation we experience in the face of a natural disaster be a function then of our own human choices?

Following the powerful 2005 hurricane that tore apart New Orleans and other neighboring counties, some experts called for a realization that the magnitude of natural disasters is best minimized by staying out of nature's way.

Dennis S. Miletti, a leading scholar on disaster prevention, pointed out that the levees in New Orleans inspired a false sense of security. "We rely on technology and we end up thinking as human beings that we're totally safe, and we're not. The bottom line is we have a very unsafe planet."

Experts: Too Many People in Nature's Way

...By one critical measure, the impact on populations, statistics show the planet to be increasingly unsafe. More than 2.5 billion people were affected by floods, earthquakes, hurricanes and other natural disasters between 1994 and 2003, a 60 percent increase over the previous two 10-year periods, U.N. officials reported at a conference on disaster prevention in January [2006].

Those numbers don't include millions displaced by last December's [2004] tsunami, which killed an estimated 180,000 people as its monstrous waves swept over coastlines from Indonesia's Aceh province to Trincomalee, Sri Lanka, and beyond.

By another measure – property damage – 2004 was the costliest year on record for global insurers, who paid out more than $40 billion (euro 31.9 billion) on natural disasters, reports German insurance giant Munich Re. Florida's quartet of 2004 hurricanes was the big factor.

But generally it's not that more "events" are happening, rather that more people are in the way, said Thomas Loster, a Munich Re expert. "More and more people are being hit," he said.

In the 1970s, only 11% of earthquakes affected human settlements, researchers at Belgium's University of Louvain report. That soared to 31% in 1993–2003, including a quake in 2003 that killed 26,000 people in Iran, whose population has doubled since the '70s.

University, April 10, 1995; http://www.darchenoam.org/ethics/PREVENT/domb1.htm.

The expanding u.s. population "has migrated to hazard-prone areas – to Florida, the Atlantic and Gulf coasts, particularly barrier islands, to California," noted retired u.s. government seismologist Robert M. Hamilton, a disaster-prevention specialist. "Several decades ago we didn't have wall-to-wall houses down the coast as we do now."

The way America builds too often invites disasters, experts say – by draining Florida swampland and bulldozing California hillsides, for example, disrupting natural runoff and magnifying flood hazards.

"We're building our communities in ways that aren't compatible with the natural perils we have," Miletti said.

The more advanced the nations, the bigger the blow may be.

Terry Jeggle, a u.n. disaster-reduction planner, cites the New Orleans levee system – dependent on pumps that run on electricity produced by fuel that must be transported in. One failure will lead to another along that chain.

"Complex systems invite compounding of complexity in consequences, too," said the Geneva-based Jeggle.

Experts fear more is to come....[24]

According to this analysis of the suffering experienced in the face of hurricanes, earthquakes and the like, *natural disasters* might better be viewed as *natural phenomena that have become disasters* as a result of bad planning and irresponsible risk taking by human beings worldwide.

Therefore, according to Rambam, one need not understand the tsunami of 2004, or Hurricane Katrina of 2005, to have carried with them messages from God. Rather, nature carries on with its course, unable to compensate for human beings' decisions to dwell in nature's path.

Powerful natural phenomena are a part of God's creation, part of the self-protection and renewal process of the earth. On the other hand, horrendous natural disasters are the result of our own bad planning.

---

24. Charles J. Hanley, "Experts: Too Many People in Nature's Way," usa *Today*, September 5, 2005; http://www.usatoday.com/weather/climate/2005-09-05-natural-disasters-worsen_x.htm. Used with permission of the Associated Press Copyright© 2010. All rights reserved.

All of this fits well into the verse from Isaiah with which we opened this chapter:

> I form light, and create darkness;
> I make peace, and create evil;
> I am the Lord, Who does all these things.[25]

One need not understand the verse to be teaching that God does evil, or that God sends evil or destruction to the world; rather, the prophet is only teaching that everything that has existed or that may potentially exist in the world, from light to dark, from peace to evil – everything was put into the world by the one God.

In fact, a close reading of the verse within its context makes it clear that this is the real point of the verse:

> I am the Lord, and there is none else,
> Beside Me there is no God;
> I have girded you, though you do not know Me;
>
> That they may know from the rising of the sun [east],
> And from the west,
> That there is none beside Me;
> I am the Lord, and there is no other;
>
> I form light, and create darkness;
> I make peace, and create evil;
> I am the Lord, Who does all these things.[26]

Reading the verse in its complete context, it is clear that its point is to convey to the reader a powerful monotheistic message. Isaiah is prophesizing about the future redeemer of the Jewish people, the Babylonian king Cyrus. He is promising Cyrus that it is God Who will ensure his victories. Although Cyrus will be born an idolater, he will recognize the greatness of the one God of Israel, and he will be introduced to God's omnipotence, God's part in all that has or is yet destined to happen.

It is in this context that Isaiah points out that peace and evil, as well as everything in between these two extremes, all come from God. God created

---

25. Isaiah 45:7.
26. Isaiah 45:5–7.

the potential for peace, as well as the potential for evil. God has given us the freedom to choose either path, and He will give that same choice to Cyrus. That choice itself is a God-given privilege.

This passage need not be understood as teaching that both peace and evil come about in this world through God's directive; rather, the verse is teaching us that the potential for peace as well as the potential for evil are choices that the one and only God of the universe has crafted and made a part of human existence.

As partners in the evolving story of this world, we are at all times able to make choices in either direction. That is what God intended. In this chapter of the Tanach, God wants Cyrus to know very clearly that his choice in this matter is also God-given. Doing evil will not align Cyrus with an adversarial power, a god that stands in opposition to the God of Israel. There is only one, all-powerful God. No other.

In this chapter, we have been exposed to more than one time-honored Jewish approach to God's role in suffering. According to one approach, God sends upon us what we perceive as evil or suffering for a specific reason; every calamity in our lives is meaningful and purposeful. According to this approach, even large-scale natural disasters should be understood to be punishments of a national or even global proportion.

However, there is another overarching approach to evil and suffering. What we perceive as evil in our lives may originate from one of three sources: (1) the results of our general susceptibility to the elements related to our fragile human condition; (2) the results of choices made by other human beings, choices that are outside of our own personal control; (3) the results of our own inadvertent choices.

It is the last of these three categories that Rambam suggests to be the most prevalent cause of the suffering we experience. Likewise, natural disasters that bring in their wake great destruction and loss of life should also be understood in this way, with the recognition that the high degree of suffering is often the direct consequence of human choice to set up residence in locations known to be situated in harm's way.

Chapter 6

CAN'T GOD PREVENT BAD THINGS
FROM HAPPENING TO GOOD PEOPLE?

**Your eyes are too pure to look on evil;
You cannot tolerate wrong.**

Why then do You tolerate the treacherous?

**Why are You silent while the wicked
swallow up those more righteous
than themselves?**

(Habakkuk 1:13)

On June 25, 2006, Itamar resident Eliyahu Asheri, age eighteen, was kidnapped by Palestinian terrorists from the Popular Resistance Committees (PRC) while hitchhiking. Four days later his lifeless body was found in the city of Ramallah. It is believed that he was murdered shortly after his kidnapping. He was shot at short range with a handgun.

Thousands of people attended the funeral of Eliyahu Asheri in Jerusalem.

"I have one big request for you, Eliyahu," his mother Miriam said. "When you stand before God, please defend the people of Israel in all its actions."[1]

According to Miriam, "What strengthens you, first of all, is knowing that everything is from God, knowing that to die sanctifying God's name, as he did – that God chose him to sanctify the name of heaven in public. This is the thing that comforts us. Any other comfort is trivial in my estimation; it doesn't let my spirit rest."[2]

---

1. *Jerusalem Post*, June 30, 2006.
2. Ibid.

On Tuesday, July 13, 2005, Nofar Horowitz, age sixteen, was killed by a suicide bomber at the entrance to the HaSharon Mall in Netanya. At her funeral the next day, her sister Reut, age seventeen, said, "You were a gift to us. You know, God only takes the good ones." At the same funeral, eulogies and prayers were punctuated by occasional wails of "Why, God, why?"[3]

Two Israeli teenagers; two funerals. Family members search for comfort, for ways to deal with the dark tragedies that have befallen them.

A mother derives comfort by interpreting her son's murder as a public sanctification of God's name. There is no doubt that many people who read the newspaper report that day had a very difficult time identifying with these expressed feelings. How was this waste of human life, this snuffing out of youth, to be interpreted as a sanctification of God's name? And yet, for Eliyahu's mother, "any other comfort was trivial."

A mournful sister derives comfort by telling herself and others that "God only takes the good ones." Again, for many who read that article in the paper that day, they most certainly could not relate to this explanation for Nofar's murder. However, for Reut, this served as her source of comfort. And yet, as the article continues, it is clear that for others, the unanswerable question "Why, God, why?" was all that came to mind for them as they stood by and watched yet another Israeli youth prematurely laid to rest.

Everything Is God's Will

Both the good and the bad – everything is from God. Rambam articulates this tenet of Judaism as follows.

TEXT
Everything That Happens Is Deserved
It is…one of the fundamental principles of the Law of Moses our Master that it is in no way possible that He, may He be exalted, should be unjust, and that all calamities that befall men and the good things that come to men, be it a single individual or a group, all of them are determined according to that which is deserved by those concerned, through equitable judgment in which there is no injustice whatsoever. Therefore, if an individual were wounded in the hand by a thorn, which he took out immediately, this would be considered a punishment

---

3. *Jerusalem Post*, July 14, 2005.

for him. And if he received the slightest pleasure, this would be reward for him, everything according to that which he deserves.[4]

In many cases, we willingly accept that everything is from God, everything is His will. We then search for understanding, and if it is hard to come by, we may assume that the problem doesn't lie with God, it lies with us.

TEXT
Suffering Is Sent by God, So Examine Your Conduct

Raba (some say, Rav Chisda) says: If a person experiences suffering, he should examine his conduct, as it is written, "Let us search and investigate our ways, and return unto the Lord" (Lamentations 3:40).

If one examines his conduct and finds nothing objectionable, then he should attribute it to the neglect of the study of the Torah, as it is written, "Happy is the one You cause to suffer, O Lord, and out of Your Torah, You shall teach Him" (Psalms 94:12).

If one attributed it to neglect of Torah study, and still did not find this to be the cause, then he can be sure that these are sufferings of love, as it is written, "For the one whom the Lord loves, He rebukes" (Proverbs 3:12)…. The sufferings wash away all of a person's sins.[5]

Confronted with suffering, this tradition teaches that the suffering is a message; God is speaking to us through the suffering, he is indicating to us that we have fallen short of His expectations. "Examine your conduct," says God. "This suffering that you are experiencing is meaningful. I am communicating to you through the suffering, and it is up to you to introspect and interpret my message."

Rabbi Benjamin Blech, in analyzing this Talmudic passage, suggests

---

4. Rambam, *Guide for the Perplexed* III:17. Rambam continues in the subsequent chapter of the *Guide* to explain that in the chapter quoted above he described the ideal situation, as divine providence relates directly to the person who has achieved spiritual perfection; however, one who is not on that level has a lesser degree of personal providence, and his sufferings and pleasure are not necessarily directly related to his actions. This position of Rambam will be further considered in chapter 7.
5. Babylonian Talmud, Berachot 5a.

that "if you are that individual who is suffering, you do have an obligation to ask yourself: What might I have done to deserve this? What could I have done to bring this on? Is it possible that my suffering is perhaps a message, a wake-up call to which I must respond?"[6] Blech goes on to emphasize that although this is the correct response to our own personal suffering, the proper response to the suffering of others is to be compassionate, not judgmental.

The concept of "sufferings of love," offered by the Talmud as a last-resort explanation, is quite difficult to embrace. According to this notion, sometimes misfortune will befall a person for no specific reason other than to increase his reward. That is to say, he will suffer in this world so that in the world to come, he will receive rewards that far outweigh his actual merits.[7]

An interesting twist on this time-honored Jewish approach to explaining suffering was offered by Rambam, who pointed out that there is actually no text in the Torah to support this approach, and that it was simply appropriated from the Arab culture of that period by our sages who found it to be meaningful.[8]

The Death of a Child

In 1981, four years following the tragic death of his oldest child, Rabbi Harold Kushner, an American Conservative rabbi, wrote a short book that became an acclaimed international bestseller. Translated into fourteen languages, it is considered a must-read for modern, God-fearing people of all religions who are looking for comfort in the face of despair, searching for God where He seems to be absent.

When faced with the death of his son Aaron, who at the mere age of fourteen succumbed to the progressive effects of a rare disease, Kushner writes that he was "compelled by a personal tragedy to rethink everything he had been taught about God and God's ways."[9]

When he first received the news as to his son's prognosis, Aaron was only three years old. "How does one handle news like that?" he writes. "How could this be happening to my family? If God existed, if He was minimally

---

6. Blech, *If God Is Good*, 17.
7. Rashi, ad loc., "*yisurim shel ahavah.*"
8. Rambam, *Guide for the Perplexed* III:17.
9. Harold Kushner, *When Bad Things Happen to Good People* (New York: Avon Books, 1981), 1.

fair, let alone loving and forgiving, how could He do this to me? And even if I could persuade myself that I deserved this punishment for some sin of neglect or pride that I was not aware of, on what grounds did Aaron have to suffer?... It simply didn't make sense."[10]

Essentially, Kushner was facing head-on a crisis in belief, and ultimately he realized that it was the result of the inherent conflicts in the way we are taught to understand God according to the following three attributes:

- **Omniscience:** God is all-knowing, continuously aware of every movement by every person on earth. Thus God is aware of a tragedy as or before it happens.

- **Omnipotence:** God is all-powerful; He is capable of performing any act, even those that violate the laws of nature. The first few chapters of Genesis tell how God created an entire universe by simply speaking it into existence. Thus God is certainly able to intrude into the world and prevent a tragedy.

- **Omnibenevolence:** God is all-loving; He cares for the world, human beings, and all other life forms that He created. Thus, as human beings, we expect God to prevent tragedy.

Belief in this triad of attributes is severely challenged when we are faced with what we interpret as unfair or undeserved suffering, i.e., in the case of the suffering or death of a child.

- If God is all-knowing, then why didn't He see what was happening to my child?

- If God is all-powerful, then why didn't He intervene to spare him this suffering?

- If God is all-loving, then why did He allow this to happen? Doesn't He care?

Is God Really All-Powerful?

In the final analysis, Kushner's journey led him to reject the belief in God's omnipotence and to resolve his own crisis in faith in a different way. Through examination of his life and the suffering of his innocent teenage son, there was no explaining what had happened. There was no explaining

---

10. Ibid., 2–3.

the disease and the degrading course it took in snuffing out his son's life. And the extent of the suffering was too great for him to accept as falling into the category of "sufferings of love."

Instead, Kushner took another approach, which at the time seemed to be the only logical way of dealing with his son's demise while at the same time maintaining his own personal belief in God. The theodicy paradox can only be solved, he determined, by redefining the attributes of God.

Viewing God as all-knowing, all-loving, and all-powerful leads to internal contradictions; in Kushner's view, at least one attribute has to be abandoned. Kushner came to the conclusion that we have no choice but to discard our belief in the *omnipotence* of God, and instead, believe in a deity with only limited powers to influence people's actions, but who remains all-knowing and all-loving.

On September 11, 2001, Kushner's God didn't prevent the terrorists because He didn't have the power to do so.

On December 26, 2004, God didn't prevent the Indian Ocean tsunamis, because God didn't have the power to do so.

On July 13, 2005, God didn't spare Nofar Horowitz, age sixteen, nor Eliyahu Asheri, age eighteen, on June 25, 2006, both killed by Palestinian terrorists, because God didn't have the power to do so.

✕ In fact, God can do no more than to weep with the victims and the families they left behind.

Kushner chose to give up on one of the three basic attributes that have always been associated with God, rather than completely give up his faith in the Divine ⌊thus understanding God as all-knowing and all-loving, but incapable of preventing suffering. ⌉

"God would like people to get what they deserve in life, but He cannot always arrange it," he writes.[11] "If God is a God of justice and not of power, then He can still be on our side when bad things happen to us."[12]

I, like so many others who have read these words, just cannot accept the thesis that God is not all-powerful. For if God is not all-powerful, then what makes Him God?

Behold, I am the LORD, the God of all flesh:
is there any thing too difficult for me?[13]

---

11. Ibid., 43.
12. Ibid., 44.
13. Jeremiah 32:27.

✦ Omnipotence is a pretty important part of what makes God God.

What has become particularly disconcerting for me is that Kushner's approach has gained international recognition as a widely held "Jewish" position – not only his own personal position.

> In much of Conservative and Reform Judaism, and in some liberal wings of Protestant Christianity, God is said to be capable of acting in the world only through persuasion, and not by coercion. God makes Himself manifest in the world through inspiration and the creation of possibility, and not by miracles or violations of the laws of nature. God relinquishes his omnipotence, in order that humanity might have absolute free will. In this view, the problem of evil does not exist.[14]

Whether such a blanket statement can be made about Conservative or Reform Judaism is certainly debatable, and that is not the point of this analysis. However, it seems that Kushner's writings have made a strong impression upon people who think about and write about theodicy.

It has bothered me for years now that this is considered to be some sort of enlightened Jewish understanding of God's role in suffering. While there is much in Kushner's book that I do agree with, this particular point is in desperate need of being rearticulated.

What Is Real Omnipotence?

There is an interesting brainteaser that goes something like this:

> Can God create a rock that even He cannot pick up?
> If so, then how can He be considered all-powerful?
> If not, then too, how can He be considered all-powerful?

Resolving these kinds of riddles has been the goal of many a philosopher throughout the ages, using various mathematical and philosophical proofs. I would, however, like to offer a straightforward suggestion. My suggestion is not new, and I realize it is open to critique, but at the same time it just makes sense, and it seems to preserve God's omnipotence for those of us who find it difficult to conceive of God otherwise.

---

14. Wikipedia, "Omnipotence," http://en.wikipedia.org/wiki/Omnipotence.

God's omnipotence describes the power to do what God *wants* to do, not the power to do what He is *capable* of doing.

You see, God is capable of doing anything and everything; however, *what makes God truly all-powerful is that He can also choose when to intervene, and when not to intervene.*

Thucydides, the great Athenian historian (471–400 BCE), wrote, "Of all the manifestations of power, restraint impresses men most."

TEXTS
Suffering Results When God Holds Back

Vespasian [the Roman emperor who ordered the destruction of the Second Temple in Jerusalem in 70 CE] sent Titus [his general], who said, "Where is their God, the rock in whom they trusted?" (Deuteronomy 32:37).

This was the wicked Titus who blasphemed and insulted heaven. What did he do? He took a harlot by the hand and entered the Holy of Holies, spread out a scroll of the Law and had sexual relations upon it. He then took a sword and slashed the curtain. Miraculously blood spurted out, and he thought that he had slain himself....

Abba Chanan said: "Oh God, Lord of multitudes, who is mighty like You, O powerful God?"(Psalms 89:9). The verse should be read as: Who is like You, mighty in self-restraint? For You heard the blaspheming and insults of that wicked man and yet You kept silent!

In the school of Rabbi Yishmael it was taught: "'Who is like You among the gods [*elim*]?' (Exodus 15:11). This verse should be read as: 'Who is like You among the silent [lit., mute] ones [*illemim*].'"[15]

Oh Lord, who is like you among the silent ones, O Lord, who is like you, for You hear the suffering of Your children and yet you are silent, as it is written in Isaiah, "For a long time I have held my peace, I have been still and restrained myself... (42:14)."[16]

---

15. Babylonian Talmud, Gittin 56b.
16. Midrash Mechilta d'Rabbi Yishmael, Tractate Shirata, chap. 8. This collection of midrash expresses the teachings of Rabbi Yishmael.

Reading between the lines of these two rabbinic texts, it appears that even the rabbis' faith was challenged by the same doubt with which we grapple: although great may have been God's intervention in the course of past events – throughout the course of history for that matter – we seem to be left with no assurance of similar interventions in the present and the future. For those who lived through the destruction of the Second Temple in Jerusalem in 70 CE, and for the following generations who experienced its aftermath, faith in God was being seriously challenged. For both Abba Chanan and Rabbi Yishmael, the events of the first and second century were filled with pain and suffering. Where was God? Had He disappeared? Was He unaware of what was happening to His people?

Abba Chanan and Rabbi Yishmael offer a different perspective on God's power, a perspective that helped them to cope. They suggest that God's real power, that which makes Him all-powerful, is His ability to control Himself in the face of grave injustices perpetrated by human beings against other human beings. God's omnipotence is manifest in His capacity to show restraint.

What makes this trait so commendable? Wouldn't we rather live in the presence of a divine being Who intervenes more often than not, Who saves and protects those who do not deserve to suffer?

We are still left therefore with the faith-shattering question: If God can intervene, but doesn't, then what makes God so great? Where is His loving-kindness?

- How could God let an innocent child die?

- How could God stand by while the Romans wreaked havoc and destruction on the Jewish people?

- How could God have allowed the Nazis to commit such evil?

- How did God let thousands die in the Twin Towers at the hands of fanatic terrorists?

I would suggest that although these are the questions that bother us, they are the wrong questions to be asking. Questions like these imply that it is God's role to intervene and protect humankind from suffering and catastrophe. It is this assumption that lies at the very foundation of our misgivings about God's power, which lead us to question His ability to prevent misfortune.

Of course God has the power to intervene, but that's not His role. Instead of asking why God does not intervene, we should rather be asking *why should He?*

Created in the Image of God

When the Torah describes God's plan to create humankind, it reveals God's plan for us from the very beginning: "And God created humankind in His image, in the image of God He created him… (Genesis 1:27)."

What does it mean to be created in the image of God? One Torah commentator, Rabbi Meir Simcha of Dvinsk (1843–1926), explained it in this way:

> To be created in the image of God [*b'tzelem Elokim*] is to be created with freedom of choice, unbound by compulsory instinct, with independent will and intellect. For the purpose of providing us with freedom of choice, God holds back His divine power. The Holy One, Blessed be He, allows room for His creations to do that which they so choose, and keeps what would be His decree or decision out of their personal choice. [He allows] humankind the freedom to choose to do good or bad as his soul desires, the ability to do things against his own natural disposition, and in opposition to that which is right in the eyes of God.[17]

These words reflect a profound idea. If this is what it means to be created in the image of God, then we might suggest the following:

1. God's power *is* limitless.

2. When God created us, He created us in His image, thereby choosing to curtail, to restrain, the extent to which He influences our lives.

3. Thus, God defined His role in our lives from the very beginning of creation: He will not interfere with our independence.

What this means to me is that many people have a mistaken understanding of God's role in our lives. While it is absolutely true that God *can* do anything and everything, it is also true that from the time He first created human beings, He purposefully limited His role; He established His role as a noninvasive one.

---

17. Rav Meir Simcha Kohen, *Meshech chochmah* (Jerusalem: Export Book Project, 1978), 2.

Writes the Meshech Chochmah: "*He allows humankind the freedom to choose to do good or bad as his soul desires.*"

What does this mean? Rambam put it this way:

> It is a fundamental principle of the law of Moses our Master, peace be upon him, and of all those who follow it that man has an absolute ability to act; I mean to say that in virtue of his nature, his choice, and his will, he may do everything that it is within the capacity of man to do, and this without there being created for his benefit in any way any newly produced thing.... This is a fundamental principle which – praise be to God – no disagreement has ever been heard in our religious community.[18]

Blech also addresses the importance of freedom of choice in his book. There he writes:

> If God were to prevent every person from doing something if it might cause an innocent to suffer, it would mean that God would have to protect good people at the expense of the principle of free will. Given the choice, God chooses to have no choice. I call this the "principle of greater priority." God's priority is that man should have free will.[19]

I understand Blech's point, but I see it very differently. I have a hard time thinking of God being "stuck between a rock and a hard place" as Blech seems to describe it. That is to say, according to Blech, God has various concerns when it comes to humankind, but His main concern is that we continue to have freedom of choice, and so God steps aside and lets things happen in order to preserve our freedom of choice and the consequences of that freedom.

Having established this, Blech then goes on to make a very provocative delineation between death by murder and death by accident. He writes:

> Now if a person makes a choice to murder another human being, he may very well succeed. Yet, it is quite possible, if not probable, that God did not want the victim to die. This has very important bearing on why bad things happen to good people....

---

18. Rambam, *Guide for the Perplexed* III:17.
19. Blech, *If God Is Good*, 31.

The man who commits murder is clearly exercising his free will. The man who kills accidentally is not.… *It is only the death by accident that is the will of God; death by intentional murder is not.*[20]

How can Blech suggest that it is so simple?

I wholeheartedly agree with him that a murder may not have been the will of God; however, why is it so clear that one who dies by accident has been subjected to God's will?

Given the principles Blech sets up, he has no choice but to conclude this. He assumes that an accidental death is not the direct result of freedom of choice, and so therefore it cannot be considered to be a product of the "principle of greater priority."

However, I would argue that the decisions to drive a car, to fly on a plane, or to work on a roof are also products of freedom of choice. The fact that they lead to death can also therefore be considered to be the result of that same choice. Why not agree that here too God would choose not to interfere with that choice, even though He knows that it will lead to the untimely death of the traveler or the builder?

In addition, Blech's commitment to the "principle of greater priority" as his explanation for why certain tragedies occur without God preventing them leaves him with the troubling question as to how God can preserve justice in the world under such circumstances. Assuming that it is God's role to maintain the balance of justice in the world, then how can we understand the innumerable injustices committed in the world every day?

In his book, Blech addresses the real-life dilemma of a rabbi he knows who, together with his wife, was seriously injured by a drunk driver. Concluding that the accident happened as a result of God's resistance to interfere with the drunk driver's choice to drive recklessly, and that the rabbi and his wife were not deserving of this suffering, Blech boldly declares the following:

> The answer, of course, is that God *must* get involved. God "owes" the rabbi. God has an obligation to rectify the undeserved harm that the victim in this situation had suffered.[21]

I suppose that if forced to understand the whole dilemma in this way, we too might be led to draw this conclusion. That is to say, if people suffer

---

20. Ibid. Italics are mine.
21. Ibid., 34.

unjustly only because God wants to give priority to freedom of choice, and if God would have certainly intervened to prevent the trauma to the rabbi and his wife if not for this priority, then what is fair is fair, and we should be able to demand that God rectify the resulting injustices of His policy.

However, the approach of Rabbi Meir Simcha of Dvinsk is not simply about giving priority to freedom of choice. His approach is far more profound, and far more compelling. The Meshech Chochmah writes that when God created human life, He determined from the very start that He would limit His involvement in our lives. Not only in order to preserve our right to choice, but for the purpose of an even higher value – that of maintaining His commitment to creating every one of us in His own image, *b'tzelem Elokim*.

Returning to the Garden of Eden

Being created in the image of God implies that we have been empowered to make fateful choices. We have been fashioned to make decisions that will impact upon our own destiny and, at times, upon the destiny of many others. This is not about preserving our freedom to choose – it is about God's ongoing commitment to honoring the *tzelem Elokim*, the inseparable spark of the Divine that resides within each and every one of us.

In fact, along these lines, I think that we have misunderstood the main messages of the first chapters of the Book of Genesis. Most of us read the story of the Garden of Eden, the eating of the fruit from the Tree of Knowledge and the subsequent expulsion from Paradise, as a story of sin and punishment, a story of shame. I would suggest that we reconsider the episode as a tale about the ageless human desire to be like God, and the natural consequences of that yearning.

It all begins with the verse we have already cited. God created humankind in His image by giving Adam and Eve the freedom to make their own personal choices. In other words, they would not be compelled to take action, forced through instinct to eat, drink, or procreate. Rather, they would be given the privilege to choose to do so.

If for instance wheat did not satisfy their tastes, they could choose to invest in grinding the wheat, making flour, adding water, allowing the dough to rise, kindling a fire, and baking bread. Though this process requires a lot more work on our part, we can choose to invest in the baking of bread or cake in order to increase the pleasure of the eating experience.

Blessed with the ability to choose to eat one way over another, we are more like God, less like animals. For this reason, God filled the garden with a vast variety of beautiful trees, pleasant to look at and good to eat. And He blessed us with a sophisticated understanding of the differences, the options. Options lead us to preferences, and preferences lead to uniqueness; not every person would have the same tastes. Each human being would develop his own unique likes and dislikes, setting him apart from the rest. Similarly, God took Adam around the garden and introduced him to all of the animals. Adam named them, valuing each animal's uniqueness, but Adam also understood that he was not an animal – he had been created differently, and he enjoyed a superior nature that was not governed by base animal instinct, but rather by choice and preference.

We have been blessed to choose our partners, to build relationships that include intimacy and love, care and concern, kindness and respect. It is this element of choice that enables us to eat, drink, and even engage in sexual relations in a godly manner.

Humankind, however, from the outset, would not be satisfied with the blessing of choice. And of course, God our Creator knew that to be the case. God knew that we would yearn to take the next step, not only to choose between options, to choose better over good, but to obtain the capacity to reason, to weigh the pros and cons of a situation, and then to expand our choices to include even the possibility of choosing bad over good, willing to suffer the potential consequences of such a decision. To be even more like God, we would long to actualize another latent God-like ability, the capacity to decide for ourselves what is good and what is bad, who is righteous and who is evil, and to act upon our decisions. This privilege would even at times put decisions of life and death in our own hands.

Instructed to refrain from eating of the fruit of the Tree of Knowledge, it was only a matter of time before Adam and Eve would choose nonetheless to do so. In fact, I would suggest that it is specifically for this reason that God put the tree there in the first place. It was not something mystical in the fruit of the tree that "opened our eyes." The decision to act against God's will led Adam and Eve to the realization that humankind has the ability to take that step and act outside of the stated will of our Creator.

This sudden discovery caused Adam and Eve to find themselves unnerved and even panic-stricken. However, the tree was strategically placed in the garden so that humankind would not only take that next step, activating our God-given ability to reason and decide what to do, but so that we would immediately learn that all such decisions will be accompanied by consequences. At times, these consequences will occur naturally; at other times, God may intervene to bring them about. In either case, these consequences will change our lives forever, and we will need to adjust to the changes we have brought about.

And so, it is no coincidence that it was the snake, the *nachash*, who enticed Eve to eat of the forbidden tree and then give to Adam as well. What the *nachash* actually did was pique Eve's interest, enticing her to reason, to be analytic, to be independent, and to think for herself. It persuaded her to reconsider – "Does it really make sense that you will die if you eat from this one tree? Look, God Himself called it the Tree of Knowledge of Good and Evil. Doesn't it make more sense to assume that God knows something you don't: namely, that when you take this next step, you will come to a new realization about yourselves? You will be empowered to decide what is good and what is bad. God has no intention of killing you! He actually wants you to eat from the tree! That is why He has made it so intriguing!"

In another context, much later on in Genesis, the Hebrew root of the word *nachash* reappears. Its usage there is very helpful in understanding the role of the snake in Eden.

Joseph, now serving as second to Pharaoh in Egypt, had plotted to frame his younger brother Benjamin with the theft of Joseph's silver goblet. (The reasons for this ruse are beyond the scope of this discussion.) When Benjamin is caught with the goods, Joseph exclaims,

> What did you think you were doing? Didn't you know that a person like myself could figure these things out [*ki nacheish yenacheish*]?[22]

In explaining these words, Rashi elaborates:

> Are you not aware that so distinguished a person as myself knows how to determine these things, to discover by way of my own intelligence and common sense or by logical deduction that it was you who stole the goblet?![23]

Joseph uses the expression *nacheish yenacheish* in reference to his ability to reason by way of intelligence, to deduce and to discover the truth for himself.

I suggest that this is what the snake, the *nachash* of the Garden of Eden,

---

22. Genesis 44:15.
23. Rashi on Genesis 44:15.

represents: the capacity to use one's own intelligence to discern right from wrong, good from evil. From the moment humankind was created in the image of God, it was known by God that such would be our preference. The *nachash* is the messenger in the story who brings to the attention of Adam and Eve that they have been empowered to make their own decisions, that deciding as to what is good and what is bad, what is right and what is wrong, is actually a privileged feature of being created in God's image. They have realized this privilege and they will now be subject to the consequences of their decision.

The Tree of Knowledge was not necessarily a test. Again, there was nothing in its fruit that radically changed humankind. Rather, it was a means through which God enabled the first human beings to explore their capacity for judgment. It taught them that when they use their God-like privilege of reason and discernment, they – by nature of their humanity – will at times choose erroneously, and will then perforce suffer the consequences.

> The woman saw that the tree was good to eat and pleasant to the eyes, and that the tree was desirable as a means to gaining intelligence. She took some of its fruit and ate. She also gave some to her husband, and he ate. The eyes of both of them were opened, and they realized they were naked. They sewed together fig leaves and made themselves loincloths.[24]

Adam and Eve did not fall from grace as a result of their decision; rather, they learned a difficult lesson about this dimension of their superiority over the rest of God's creations. They took the chance, and they did not die; however, they did suffer consequences that would accompany human life throughout eternity. Among other things, God proclaimed that humankind would toil in their work and that women would suffer great pain in childbirth. And then, as a final measure, God banned us from life in Paradise.

The toil of our work reminds us of our decision to have more control over our destiny. More control is accompanied by greater potential for failure and disappointment, as well as demanding of us a greater investment of effort.

Pain in childbirth reminds us of the significant consequences of

---

24. Genesis 3:6–7.

choosing to partner with God in the creation and preservation of human life. The pain and even the danger that women experience when giving birth serve as a reminder of the agonizing choices that accompany our privileged role on earth as the developers and the guardians of the earth. Our role as human beings does not end when we have successfully procreated human life; in fact, endowing another human being with an awareness of the power of choice is an essential part of our mission.

After we actualized our choice to play a greater role in our destinies, to utilize the privilege of reasoning, choosing, reaping benefits, and suffering consequences, life in Paradise no longer suited our needs. And therefore, banishment was not necessarily a punishment, but simply an essential adjustment that would enable us to discover what we were looking for. The hovering sword guarding the entrance to the garden, as described in the Torah,[25] reminds us that for as long as we live, a paradise-like existence is off-limits to us, for it is not in line with living a life laden with responsibilities and challenges.

The *keruvim*, the two angelic figures who guard the path to the Tree of Life, are said to have childlike faces. Like the *keruvim* that would ultimately grace the cover of the Holy Ark in the Temple, they remind us of our limits. They remind us that in our "youth," at the very beginning of our human existence, we chose to be more God-like, we chose to take upon ourselves greater responsibility. For this reason, the Tree of Life is off-limits – again, not as a punishment, and not because eating from its fruit would in some way make us a threat to God. But, just as God says, "Behold, humankind has become as one of Us, knowing good and evil; and now, lest he put forth his hand and also take from the Tree of Life, and eat and live forever,"[26] he must be banished from the garden. That is to say, if human beings are to espouse the role to which they aspire, they must remain mortal. Only a mortal can take risks. Only a mortal can wipe out disease and take great pride in that achievement. Only a mortal will be privileged to be involved in life and death decisions, to seek solutions, to celebrate achievements, to suffer consequences.

And so, the story of Eden is not a tragic tale of rebellion against God's instruction; rather, it is a lesson about humankind's empowerment to encounter decisions of a more complex variety. Upon eating from the Tree

---

25. Genesis 3:24.
26. Genesis 3:32.

of Knowledge, the issue facing humanity shifted from simply choosing between options – some good, some better. Suddenly, humanity was charged with making risky, consequence-laden decisions, which could result in great successes or grave consequences. As human beings, we are not satisfied with choosing good based solely on what we are told; we yearn for the privilege of deciding for ourselves, knowing full well that such choices can be to our detriment. Nonetheless, the privilege of considering and choosing, the privilege of further emulating God's ways, is worth the potential consequences involved in such choices, even the potential suffering that may come about in the wake of such decisions.

Therefore, the saga of the Garden of Eden reinforces for us our belief that God is all-powerful. Yet, in order to give us the privilege of living our lives in His image, God deliberately established limitations to His own involvement in our lives. He blessed us with the ability to discern and taught us that our decisions could have tragic, even catastrophic consequences. Out of His infinite love, He shared with us this capacity to choose. As a demonstration of His infinite power, He continues to restrain Himself from directing our decisions or deflecting the consequences of those decisions, for that is the role He ascribed for Himself from the very beginning.

God and the Drunk Driver

I therefore disagree with Blech's suggestion that God "owes" the suffering rabbi, or that He has some sort of obligation to rectify the situation. When the drunk driver smashed into this couple, it is possible to surmise that:

1. The rabbi and his wife did not deserve the suffering that ensued.

2. Nonetheless, God did not intervene, even though He could have, because that is not the role He established for Himself at the time of His creation of humankind.

3. Although God may, out of a benevolent sense of mercy and compassion, certainly choose to rectify the situation, He is not in any way obligated to do so.

In summary, according to this alternate approach, we are saying that God is supremely powerful, all-knowing, and beneficent. God knows our most intimate thoughts, is well aware of all of our actions, and manages our destiny in response to the choices we make or others make for us.

The text and counter-text presented in this chapter offer two very different rabbinic approaches to suffering. The first text articulated the approach that views all suffering as sent by God to make a point, and that it is our responsibility to search for meaning within suffering. The second text indicates that suffering comes about because God restrains Himself from micromanaging, from intervening in the course of our lives. I have suggested that this could be the result of our having been created in the image of God, empowered to make choices and to suffer the consequences of those choices.

According to this second approach, assuming that it is not God's role to intervene in our lives, then why do we pray to Him for assistance, to perform miracles for us? What can we hope to accomplish with even the most fervent of petitions?

The answer to this question may lie in the way we choose to define a miracle.

Chapter 7

WHERE'S MY MIRACLE?

My Miracle Escape

"The bomber was one meter away from me, inside my store. It was a miracle – there is a creator of this world," said Itzik Sharon, one of the owners of the shwarma stand at the old central bus station in Tel Aviv, where a suicide bomber wounded 27 on Thursday afternoon.

"A guy walked in holding nothing," said Sharon, 36, minutes before being released from Ichilov Hospital just two hours after the attack. "He looked suspicious, holding his hands in his pockets. I turned my head the other way, and within seconds I heard a blast."

According to Sharon, there were between 15 and 20 people at the stand when the attack occurred. After making sure his twin brother was not hurt, Sharon said he looked for a way out. The first phone call he made was to his wife.

"Thank God, we are all healthy, and we are going to continue," he said. "Leaving the hospital is the best possible feeling."

"What saved me was the Book of Psalms I've had in my bag for the past two weeks," said Ben Friedman, 29, a construction worker who said he stopped at the shwarma stand regularly on his way home from work.

Minutes before the attack, Friedman, who said he was in the process of becoming religious, was busy thinking about the new apartment he was supposed to move into on Thursday evening.

"I was looking for a place to put down my pita when I heard a loud explosion and the place went dark," Friedman said. "There was a smell of death in the air, and then I saw a mangled body lying on the floor."

> After remaining frozen for two minutes, Friedman said, he crawled toward the kitchen. Having narrowly escaped a suicide attack last year at the Carmel Market in Tel Aviv minutes before it took place, Friedman said that he hoped this time he suffered nothing more than a light back wound.
>
> "I hope it's just my back, not my soul," he said, adding that images from the attack kept flashing back before his eyes.
>
> "I don't know if I'll go back there," he said. "Then again, when He is looking for you, He can find you anywhere."[1]

The years of suicide bombings and threats of suicide bombings throughout the duration of the Al-Aqsa Intifada (2000–2006) forced Israelis to confront on a regular basis the delicate issues of fate and destiny, the tragic as well as the miraculous. As I have written in previous chapters, in the face of what appears to be unjust suffering or death, people will naturally search for explanations, for ways of making sense of their dire predicament.

On January 19, 2006, the lives of Itzik Sharon and Ben Friedman were spared inside Sharon's *shwarma* stand in Tel Aviv. A Palestinian suicide bomber entered the small stand and attempted to snuff out the lives of some thirty Israelis who were dining there or standing nearby. In the end, the only life he managed to take was his own, although he did cause significant injury to many of the customers. Sharon noted that "it was a miracle," and even more, that it was proof that "there is a creator of this world."

Friedman too noted that it was a miracle, and attributed his escape to the Book of Psalms that he had been carrying around in his knapsack.

One Man's Miracle Is Another Man's Tragedy

Whenever I come across such exclamations of thanksgiving, expressing proof of divine intervention in our lives, I can't help but look at the event from the perspective of the others, those who sustained permanent debilitating injuries in the attack – loss of an eye, or an arm or leg. I immediately think of the other families, those who are in mourning, those whose loved ones are suffering, who are reading the same article that I am reading, at that same moment – reading of Itzik's escape from the hands of death, or of Ben's Book of Psalms – and I feel their anguish as they will

---

1. Talya Halkin, "My Miracle Escape," *Jerusalem Post*, January 20, 2006. Reprinted with the permission of the *Jerusalem Post* and www.jpost.com.

ask themselves, time and again throughout their lives, amid thoughts filled with a combination of anger and sorrow, "Where's *my* miracle? Why didn't God spare *me, my* husband, *my* wife, *my* child?"

On February 1, 2003, the entire crew of the NASA space shuttle *Columbia* perished in a tragic explosion over Texas during reentry into the earth's atmosphere. Ilan Ramon, the first Israeli astronaut, was on that flight. Although Ramon described himself as a secular, nonobservant Jew, he requested special kosher meals for his journey and consulted with rabbis before leaving about the proper manner in which to observe Shabbat from space. Among the items he carried into space was a small Torah scroll rescued from the Bergen-Belsen concentration camp. The president of the State of Israel also gave Ramon a microfilm copy of the Torah to keep on him at all times during his journey.[2]

If a Book of Psalms preserved the life of Ben Friedman in the face of a terrorist attack, why didn't a Torah scroll and an additional complete copy of the Torah on microfilm protect the life of astronaut Ilan Ramon?

For some people, the notion that they have experienced a miracle while others did not creates an unbearable sense of guilt. Following the June 1, 2001, suicide bombing at the Dolphinarium in Tel Aviv, which claimed the lives of 21 young men and women and injured another 120, one sixteen-year-old girl named Tami had a very difficult time dealing with the death of one of the victims, a close friend of hers. Tami herself had only been a few blocks away from the club when the bombing took place. For months she suffered from feelings of guilt over the fact that she had survived the bombing and her close friend had not, that her life had been spared and her friend's had come to a violent end. Eventually the guilt over her escape led her to attempt suicide by jumping out of the third-story window of her aunt's Tel Aviv apartment.[3]

If Itzik Sharon's survival was a miracle, proof of God's existence, then how should we interpret the deaths of eleven hundred people by Palestinian violence and terrorism during the six-year long Al-Aqsa Intifada? Was not a single one of those people sufficiently deserving of a miracle? Do those tragic deaths stand to prove that God doesn't exist?

---

2. Nissan Ratzalav-Katz and Ezra HaLevi, "Israel Remembers Fallen Astronaut and War Hero Ilan Ramon," *Israel National News*, February 2, 2007; http://www.israelnationalnews.com/News/News.aspx/120745.

3. *Jerusalem Post*, March 14, 2007.

I do not mean to imply that personal miracles don't occur – I certainly believe that they do! Nor do I suggest that those who have escaped great danger have not been the beneficiaries of God's protection. God is all-powerful and can certainly intervene. But the implication of claiming that one person's rescue was a miraculous godsend leads directly to the question as to why that person *deserved* to be rescued and another person did not. It's this issue of *deserving* that I wish to address in this chapter.

What Constitutes a Miracle?

Before we tackle the big questions concerning what makes one person worthy of miraculous intervention and another person not, or under what circumstances God does intervene and when He does not, let's first seek to better define the concept of a miracle.

The thirteenth-century Torah scholar Ramban suggested that there are two types of miracles, both of them the result of God's direct involvement in our lives.

The first type constitutes those miracles that appear to be supernatural. These we call signs or wonders (*otot* or *moftim*). All of the biblical promises of reward for proper behavior and the warnings regarding punishment in the wake of transgression must be interpreted as signs and wonders. It is not natural that the heavens should give forth rain in their due season as a result of our observance of *mitzvot*, nor that they should hold back rain as a result of our sins.

In addition, there is a second type of miracle: every natural occurrence is really a bona fide divine intervention in our lives – it's just that since such interventions don't appear to upset the natural order, we don't acknowledge them as miraculous. Essentially, there are only miracles; nothing is just the result of mere natural consequences, cause and effect, or the ways of the world.[4] Miracles are happening for us at all times, but we are just not aware of them.[5]

In our previous chapter, based on a teaching of the nineteenth-century commentator Rabbi Meir Simcha of Dvinsk, we developed a very different approach. To review, I suggested there that according to the role that God established for Himself from the very beginning, God is not inclined to

---

4. Ramban in his commentary on the Torah, Genesis 17:1, 46:15.
5. Rashi, Shabbat 13b, s.v. *"ein shoteh nifga."*

get involved in managing our lives, in directing our decisions or deflecting their consequences. Of course, He still retains the prerogative to do so, but only exercises this right under certain circumstances. Otherwise, He allows us to act freely, and subsequently to reap the benefits or suffer the consequences of our actions.

In other words, there are natural consequences to our actions in this world; not everything that happens to us has been decreed from above. Rambam made this point clear when he referred to the difference between the Greek philosophers and the Jewish sages.

> The philosophers said that God's will is to be found in everything that happens, every decision that is made, every action and every reaction.
>
> We don't believe that. Rather, we believe that God's will was made clear during the six days of creation, that all things would just continue to function from that time on according to their nature…. For when a person stands or sits and says that it is the will of God, may He be blessed, that he stand or sit, he means to say that God included in nature from the beginning that a person will stand or sit according to his own choice – not that it is God's will at that specific moment that he do so.[6]

First-Order Miracles versus Second-Order Miracles

Of course, it is important to realize that even at times when God is not intervening directly, natural consequences are also an aspect of His divine will, His providence in our lives. To understand better how this might work, let's consider the difference between two types of miracles. I will refer to these two categories as others have: first-order miracles and second-order miracles.

TEXT
The World Pursues Its Natural Course
Philosophers asked the elders in Rome, "If your God has no desire for idolatry, why does He not abolish it?" They replied, "If it was something of which the world has no need that was worshipped, He would abolish it; but people worship the sun, moon, stars, and planets. Should He destroy the universe on

---

6. Rambam, "Introduction to Tractate Avot," chapter 8.

account of fools?! Instead, the world pursues its natural course, and as for the fools who act wrongly, they will have to render an account."

Another illustration: Suppose a man stole a measure of wheat and went and sowed it in the ground; it is right that it should not grow, but the world pursues its natural course, and as for the fools who act wrongly, they will have to render an account.

Another illustration: Suppose a man has intercourse with his neighbor's wife; it is right that she should not conceive, but the world pursues its natural course, and as for the fools who act wrongly, they will have to render an account.[7]

According to this important text, there is a natural order that is ever-present in our lives, a natural course that adheres to certain rules and principles. "The world pursues its natural course" indicates that there are set laws in nature, and these laws are normally neither suspended nor superseded. Why should an adulteress conceive a child? It's not right. It's not fair. The same could be said in the case of a woman who was raped. But in fact, says the Talmud, she may very well conceive as a result of the natural order of the world. Life will run its course, but the transgressors will not be forgotten. Someday, each and every one of them will pay dearly for their actions. God will be sure to even the score, for no action goes unnoticed, no evil goes unaddressed. Meanwhile, however, unspeakable events will unfairly transpire without God's intervention. He will not decree them, nor will He prevent them. God will allow human beings to perpetrate these acts and He will allow the acts to follow their natural course because God honors the terms of creation, the natural course of the world.

And that too is providential. It is an expression of first-order miracles in our world.

First-order miracles comprise all of the processes set in motion by God in the natural world from the very beginning. Plants produce oxygen and eliminate carbon dioxide through photosynthesis. The sun rises and sets at predictable times day after day, year after year, producing dramatic natural spectacles at which we marvel. Gravity, the force that attracts a body toward the center of the earth, enables us to live day-to-day in an orderly fashion.

---

7. Babylonian Talmud, Avodah Zarah 54b.

Water evaporates, rises, and forms clouds that bring rain to maintain life. The human brain processes on the order of 60,000,000,000,000,000 operations per second or higher, constantly processing billions of inputs from the skin, eyes, ears, nose, and tongue, matching those inputs to sense memory, monitoring and adjusting hormone levels, respiration, and heart rate. People crave to receive love, and seek ways to give love, leading to millions of acts of loving-kindness every day. Parents nurture their offspring to adulthood, so that they too can become parents and do the same.

All of these are examples of God's primary providence, first-order miracles, ways of the world put into motion from the very beginning and forever a part of our lives. Although we may take them for granted, they are nonetheless miracles, basic provisions without which we could not function. God put them in place and, according to the above Talmudic text, He will not normally interfere with them.

In the years following the disengagement from the Gaza Strip and the uprooting of thousands of lives, some Israelis looked to God to punish the perpetrators. Unable to fathom how God could have allowed the events of the summer of 2005 to have actually come about, believers turned their eyes and ears to current events in an effort to see the hand of God in the aftermath of disengagement. People seemed to find contentment in believing that although God did not intervene to prevent the disengagement, He would not forgive nor forget those who had carried it out.

In 2006–7, a number of political and military leaders who had been in positions of power during the events of the summer of 2005 were forced out of office. The prime minister lay in a coma; the president, the chief of staff, and others had been removed from their positions for different reasons. A newspaper story in early 2007 asked a variety of religious leaders to comment on this series of events. Was what seemed to be a clearing out of leadership to be interpreted as a manifestation of divine justice, a heavenly punishment being meted out against these individuals for their roles in the disengagement from the Gaza Strip?[8]

While opinions among the respondents varied, the majority viewed it as the hand of God, and suggested that those who could not see it as such are not seeing correctly. Said one respondent,

---

8. *BaSheva*, a predominately religious Zionist publication, no. 231 (February 2, 2007). Citations from *BaSheva* are my translation.

Although we do not understand the hidden ways of the heavenly court, and we do not know what is written in the record books of each and every individual, still, the collapse of the leaders and the governing bodies testifies definitively that the Land of Israel demands compensation for its disgrace, and that the words of the land are heard in the heavens.[9]

One respondent, however, suggested a different perspective on the ways of God, on the definition of God's intervention and God's ways of justice in our world. He responded,

If the interviewer's reference to "heavenly punishment" is meant to imply a supernatural level of intervention, my leaning is to reject this suggestion. Firstly, because it is forbidden to assume that we can manage the record books of the Holy One, blessed be He. And, in addition, among the ranks of those who were uprooted from their homes there are many who have experienced a decline in health, personal standing, etc. [Is their tragic situation then also to be judged as punishment for some sin?] On the other hand, one cannot ignore what is happening.... And therefore, I conclude that the downfall [of these officials] is neither by way of a miracle, nor is it coincidental, it is simply the natural result of the expulsion process....

If a person in his depression should jump from the top of a building, he will crash upon the ground below, not as a punishment but rather because of the laws of physics....

The nature of socio-national processes are complex. Their results are not immediate, like the laws of physics, and in addition, they are more flexible in nature and include a range of possible results. However, the socio-political laws established in our world by God are most definitely at work, and slowly but surely the results of the crime materialize and take on names and faces. One of the foundational "laws," for instance, in the laws of community, is that you cannot fool all of the people all of the time....[10]

These latter comments are very much in line with the above Talmudic text, perhaps even taking the concept one step further. Not only are our lives

9. Ibid., 5.
10. Ibid., 11.

governed by natural laws, set in place by God, that govern our physical existence, such as the laws of gravity, the laws of the harvest, or the biological laws that govern conception of human life, but we are also subject to the socio-political laws of human nature. These too were set in motion by God at the time of our creation. These socio-political laws, corrective measures built into the very fabric of human existence, are no less divine in their nature, and those who suffer the consequences of these laws or ultimately reap the benefits of these laws have also experienced the consequences of divine providence, or more specifically, a first-order miracle.

At the end of the summer of 1991, our family moved from Albany, New York, to Kansas City, Missouri. In driving out to our new home we divided up the road trip, staying overnight in a motel somewhere in Ohio. Shortly after our arrival at the motel, my wife and two sons headed to the motel's swimming pool.

My wife was playing in the water with our oldest son, who was then four years old. Meanwhile, our two-year-old son, who had been sitting on the side waiting his turn, slipped and fell into the unattended motel pool. I was getting something from our ground-floor motel room at the time. Too far away to reach him, my wife began to scream, alerting me that something was wrong.

Adrenaline, I have learned, is a "fight or flight" hormone, released from the adrenal glands whenever danger threatens. When secreted, adrenaline enters into the bloodstream to instantly prepare the body for action in emergency situations. It increases the supply of oxygen and glucose to the muscles, making a person more mentally alert and physically stronger.

It might have been the adrenaline rushing through my veins that enabled me to run from our room, faster than I had ever run before, and leap over the chain-link fence into the pool just in the nick of time.

One might say that I saved the life of our two-year-old son that day.

Unless of course, like me, you would consider the effects of adrenaline nothing less than miraculous. And if that is the case, then you might agree with me that it was God Who saved our son's life that day, not necessarily by intervening, but through the blessing of a first-order miracle.

First-order miracles are integral parts of our lives, experienced equally by all of us. Through first-order miracles God blesses us all with miraculous moments every day. In this way, God is ever-present in our lives, and His miracles abound.

Kindness and Faithfulness

In a number of places, the Book of Psalms describes God's interventions in the world using the often-combined terms of *chesed* (kindness) and *emunah* (faithfulness). For instance:

> "I will sing out that your *chesed* stands firm generation after generation, that you have established your *emunah* in heaven itself" (89:2), or

> "It is good to praise the Lord and make music to Your name, O Most High, to proclaim your *chesed* in the morning and your *emunah* at night" (92:1–2).

What is the meaning of *chesed* combined with *emunah*?

The nineteenth-century Russian rabbi and Bible commentator known as Malbim explained this important distinction in a way that very much parallels the ideas we have been considering in this chapter. He suggested that these two terms refer to two different ways in which God involves Himself in our worldly affairs, two different levels of intervention.

> ***Chesed*** is something that God does as an act of grace, without any established obligation to do so.

> ***Emunah*** describes that which God does based on a promise He once made.

For instance, the laws of nature are manifestations of *emunah*. For after God established the earth and the laws of nature, it is to be understood that there and then He promised that these laws would forever function – something we could always count on. However, when God does something that we might describe as supernatural, it is not based on any sort of obligation or promise that He made to us. It is not His responsibility to do this, and He is not to be held accountable if He does not take such action.

Malbim went one step further, adding yet another dimension to this delineation. He suggested that even natural law is programmed to behave in wondrous, supernatural ways for those who are deserving of reward, and is capable of acting destructively when encountering those who are deserving of punishment. Nature then, set in motion by God, is also sensitive to human activity, and is capable of bringing about hidden miracles according to our deeds. In other words, there is also an element of subjectivity involved in the allocation of nature's ways.[11]

I would suggest that in his commentary here, Malbim actually differentiated between first-order miracles (*emunah*) and second-order miracles (*chesed*), which we will next consider. He suggested that first-order miracles can also function at times as second-order miracles in response to the actions of human beings. The more deserving may benefit from greater portions of blessing, while the undeserving will receive lesser portions. More rain, more wheat, better health for the deserving, and drought, famine, disease for the undeserving. This, according to Malbim, is built into the natural world as well, indicating that we as human beings are much more integrated into nature than we might otherwise believe.

What We're Really Praying For: Second-Order Miracles
When we feel desperation and we turn to God in prayer for deliverance, for what are we praying? Usually we perceive that it's too late for a first-order miracle, there is no solution in the natural order of things, and the odds are against it. Therefore, we are reaching out to God in hope of being blessed with a second-order miracle.

Zion Was Praying for Divine Assistance When His Rescue Boat Came In

The food was gone, the stench of sewage and mildew unbearable. Zion Akram, who had been forced upstairs into his landlord's apartment when water deluged his own ground floor New Orleans home two days earlier, didn't know how much longer he and his three neighbors had.

"I felt I was really on the top of the cliff and it started worrying me. I woke up and realized nobody was going to help us," he recalled. So the 58-year-old retired cabbie wound tefillin around his thin, weathered arm and begged for divine assistance.

As he looked up from his prayer book, he saw a small boat float into his backyard. For one full day he watched the oarless dinghy and wondered how he could put it to use. The next morning he again lay tefillin and asked God for help. This time,

---

11. For a full discussion of these ideas see Malbim's commentary to Psalms 89:2 and 92:2.

as Akram finished his prayers, he saw a person up to his neck in feces walking by the front door.

"Are you crazy? The water is full of bacteria and disease," Akram shouted at him. But the man replied, "I'm here to help somebody." Tying the rope that he happened to carry with him to the boat, the man made three trips back and forth through the muck to bring Akram and his neighbors to safety.

"With Noah, God told him the flood was coming and to get the boat ready," noted Akram, who moved to New Orleans from his native Israel 10 years ago. "With us, the boat came to our house." Akram reflected on his "miracle" from his temporary home in Houston, estimated to hold about half of a New Orleans Jewish community that numbered close to 10,000 until Katrina struck. A week after his rescue, Akram described himself as "still tripping on my happiness."[12]

Second-order miracles are the kind of events that we normally think of when we use the word *miracle*. Zion Akram believed that he experienced a second-order miracle. These types of miracles occur as moments or incidents that defy our expectations and run counter to our assumptions:

- Surviving a head-on collision, where both cars were totaled
- Escaping unscathed from the carnage of a suicide bombing
- Praying endlessly for a child, only to conceive at the very moment when all hope was lost
- Two brothers, Holocaust survivors, reunited after more than sixty years of assuming each other to be dead
- Being saved from certain death by an unknown brave soul who appears out of nowhere

These are the miracles that make the headlines, the ones that amaze us.

Our first thought is always, "It's a miracle!"

Our second thought: "What did he do to deserve it?" We assume that a supernatural, second-order miracle can only come about for the one who merits it. The person found favor in God's eyes, and so he or she was blessed

---

12. Hilary Leila Krieger, "Zion Was Praying for Divine Assistance When His Rescue Boat Came In," *Jerusalem Post*, September 9, 2005. Reprinted with the permission of the *Jerusalem Post* and www.jpost.com.

with a miracle. The corollary to this, of course, is that one who does not merit God's miraculous intervention is, for some reason, not worthy.

Is this necessarily the case? We may need to reconsider our assumptions after reading the next Talmudic text.

COUNTER-TEXT
Reconsidering Second-Order Miracles

Our rabbis taught: It once happened that a man's wife died and left a child to be suckled, and he could not afford to pay a wet nurse, whereupon a miracle was performed for him and his breasts opened like the two breasts of a woman and he nursed his son. Rav Joseph observed, "Come and see how great was this man, that such a miracle was performed on his account!"

Said Abaye to him, "On the contrary: how lowly was this man, that the order of the creation had to be changed on his account!"

This counter-text indicates that there certainly are personal, supernatural miracles in this world. The story describes an incident of personal providence, a second-order miracle, in which God intervened in a very direct fashion to save the child, an innocent sufferer. Like so many biblical stories that begin with desperation and end in supernatural miracles, this rabbinic story teaches us that God continues to maintain a very direct, personal relationship with each and every one of us. He is aware of our needs and is willing to intervene whenever necessary.

While the previous Talmudic passage taught that even when we would wish it to be otherwise, nature must run its course and divine justice will be forthcoming in its aftermath, this passage teaches that at times God will alter the natural order of the world for the sake of providing for our needs. The child did not suffer starvation, as might have otherwise been the natural course of events.

In this counter-text, both Rav Joseph and Abaye, two fourth-century Babylonian scholars, agreed that this was a supernatural incident, and that God does intervene directly in our lives when He deems it necessary to do so. However, as amazing as this miracle may have been, Abaye stated that in the scheme of things, the greater miracle is the miracle that happens without the altering of nature. In other words, a first-order miracle is preferable to a second-order miracle.

Why is that? Isn't it just the opposite?

This Talmudic text describes a supernatural miracle, an uncommon, unprecedented detour from the course of the natural world. This teaching at once marvels at God's miracles, specifically second-order miracles, that He performs for those who are in desperate need, and at the same time recoils from the manipulation of the natural order that had to come about in order to provide for the needs of this destitute man and his motherless child.

Abaye was of the opinion that the natural order of the world, established for the purpose of maintaining life on earth, is what testifies to the greatness of God's creations. God established these natural laws and phenomena specifically to protect and preserve life, to maximize the quality of our existence, and so it is specifically the existence and stability of this natural order as it manifests itself in our life that testifies to our greatness.

I think I understand very clearly what Abaye was saying. He was teaching us that God is at all times rendering miracles for us. Miracles are a part of our everyday lives; it's just that we are looking for them in all the wrong places. We are looking for supernatural occurrences. The freaky, inexplicable events of our lives are the ones that we consider miraculous, while the day-to-day miracles of primary providence go unnoticed.

What's more, in the case of the widower and his newborn, a first-order miracle could have been provided for him. For instance, our human conscience is a first-order miracle. It directs us to do good, to sacrifice for others. Our creative and innovative abilities to envision solutions to dilemmas, to develop cures for illnesses, are all first-order miracles. Our resourcefulness in discovering new ways of extricating ourselves from the most dire of circumstances – this too is a first-order miracle.

Was the anonymous savior of Zion Akram really the deliverer of a second-order miracle? A man rose to the occasion and listened to an inner voice that called upon him to risk his own life to save others. Something came over him, and he activated the resources of altruism and humanity that are part of the makeup of every human being, a part of the image of God that serves as the foundation of our human existence.

Zion prayed for a second-order miracle, but perhaps what he was actually blessed with was a first-order miracle.

When Abaye heard that in order to provide for this baby, the natural order had to be manipulated, he reasoned that it must be that this man did not merit benefiting from the built-in powers associated with first-order miracles, acts representative of God's *emunah*, the kind of miracles that fill the world and enrich our lives at all times. Instead, God had to send a second-order miracle, a supernatural event, in order to take care of the needs of this hungry child.

Rabbi Akiva Eiger, a great rabbinic scholar of the early nineteenth century, wrote:

> A person should not pray for something which is not according to the natural order, even though such a thing is within the ability of the Holy One, blessed be He. For instance, when a woman suffers a miscarriage, one should not pray that the child live, and it is forbidden for a person to pray that the Holy One, blessed be He, perform a miracle that includes a deviation from the natural order; for instance, that a certain tree should bring forth fruit before its time.[13]

Like Abaye, this sage discouraged looking to God to disturb the natural order. Abaye argued more forcefully: if the widower had been more deserving, he would have enjoyed a miracle in a more natural way, in a way that would not have conflicted with the act of creation, i.e., by meriting greater earnings, enabling him to hire a wet nurse for his hungry son.

According to Abaye, natural is greater than supernatural, and being the beneficiary of a second-order miracle is no indication of greater merit.

Abaye's approach could be the key to understanding another enigmatic Talmudic story:

> Rav Mari the son of the daughter of Shmuel related: Once I was standing on the bank of the river Papa, and I saw angels disguised as sailors who brought sand and loaded it upon ships, and the sand turned into fine flour.
>
> When the people came to purchase it, I called out to them, "Do not buy this because it is the result of a miracle!"
>
> The next day, boatloads of wheat came from Perezina [a town near Bagdad].[14]

---

13. Notes of Rabbi Akiva Eiger, *Shulchan Aruch*, Orach Chayim, 230:1.
14. Babylonian Talmud, Taanit 24b.

There was a famine in Babylonia. What was it about the miraculous conversion of sand into fine flour that bothered Rav Mari, a third-century Babylonian scholar, so very much that he felt compelled to warn people not to eat it? Did he view it as a health hazard? Was he concerned that benefiting from the miracle-flour would require cashing-in on "merit points" that may be awaiting the people, and so he was alerting them to beware of the steep price of eating the miracle-flour?[15]

It seems to me that Rav Mari had a different concern. The warning about the miracle-flour parallels the message that Abaye would later convey in his comments about the miracle-milk.

Benefiting from a second-order miracle may suit their needs right now. In fact, not only would they be the beneficiaries of unrefined grain, but of fine flour! However, Rav Mari was not willing to settle for this. Rav Mari senses that the people deserve better!

"How could it be that these people were not deserving of a first-order miracle, one that provides from within the natural order of life, without resorting to supernatural circumstances?" he may have thought to himself. Accepting the fine flour produced by the costumed angels would be an acknowledgement of their second-rate status, of the need for exceptional emergency measures in order to deal with a unique situation.

"No," exclaims Rav Mari, "we will have none of this! Do not eat this flour! You, angels, take notice! These people are more deserving! I refuse to allow them to be considered a special case!"

And so, the story ends with what might have been misinterpreted as a simple coincidence. Lo and behold, on the very next day, boatloads of wheat arrived from overseas. What did the people think? Were they merely thankful that their needs were met, that they could make bread and feed their families? Or, did they realize that they had been the beneficiaries of a first-order miracle, as Rav Mari had insisted?

Miracles That Go Unnoticed

How often are we cognizant of the first-order miracles in our lives? How often do we simply take them for granted or chalk them up to coincidence?

When two small white tablets take away the excruciating pain of a headache, when we lose a job just to find another one that is much better

---

15. A notion expressed by Rabbi Yannai in the Babylonian Talmud, Shabbat 32a.

than the first, when we mention the name of a person whom we haven't heard from in a long time just to receive a call or run into them "out of the blue," rekindling a long-neglected friendship, when we steer away from an automobile accident just in the nick of time – all of these, I contend, are various forms of first-order miracles in our lives.

The world's natural course is really a divine, finely tuned, miraculously powerful force that surrounds us, encourages us, supports us, and protects us. It is a receptacle for many different forms of first-order miracles that accompany us through life. We merit from its infinite benefits at all times, usually not conscious of its presence in our lives. It is this natural course that God put into motion from the very beginning, and that He is committed to preserving for us, even though it means constantly restraining Himself from more overt intervention.

The Talmud records a discussion as to why people do not take note to celebrate the many times that God has come to their rescue. Unlike earlier sages who had actually listed the dates of many miraculous events that they had experienced, the rabbis in the Talmudic era neglected to do so:

> Rabban Shimon ben Gamliel observed: We too appreciate our troubles and salvation, but what can we do? For if we come to write [them down], we would not adequately keep track of them, for they are so numerous.
>
> Another reason suggested: It is because just as a fool does not perceive the troubles that surround him, so we do not perceive our miraculous escapes.[16]

As I was in the midst of writing this chapter, my eldest son and his future bride were in an automobile accident. My son came home and described the circumstances. They were crossing through an intersection and before they had made it all the way through, an oncoming car smashed into the rear end of the car, sending it into a spin, ending up in some brush on the side of the road. Their car had a small dent. The other car was totaled. No one was hurt.

In 1989, when my eldest son was just a year and a half old, he was strapped into his car seat in the back seat of our family station wagon as we drove through a blizzard on the New York State Thruway. At a certain point, the visibility suddenly became absolutely impossible, and when I

---

16. Babylonian Talmud, Shabbat 13b. My translation is based on Rashi's explanation.

attempted to maintain control by stepping on the brakes, our car went into a spin, ending up against the guardrail on the highway median. No other cars hit us, and we were towed home, no one injured.

When my wife thinks back on the accident, she sees his little innocent face, unable to comprehend what had happened. He doesn't remember the accident, but we do.

I believe that in both of these cases, as well as in the case of the motel pool, God performed a miracle for our family. Not the supernatural second-order type of miracle, but the kind that is integrated into the ways of the world. Sure, people might call it lucky, fortunate, a close call – but I like to think of these events as miracles. They are the kinds of miracles that blend in with the natural order of life; they come about through quick thinking, through a sudden surge of alertness and strength – miracles of the natural order, miracles that emanate from God's ever-present, kind providence in our lives.

How Does Prayer Work?

A university student once challenged Rabbi Hayim David HaLevy to explain how it is possible that prayer can come along and alter God's will. How can our prayers change God's mind? For example, if a person were dying, is it really possible that our prayers could lead God to decide to heal, even though His original intention was to allow the person to die?

In response, Rabbi HaLevy offered the following explanation: "Receiving the Divine influence can be compared to rain. Just as rain cannot make the earth flourish without the earth having been cultivated in advance through plowing and planting by human beings, so too, prayer and the spiritual work that goes with it cannot be helpful without prior preparation. A man cannot pray for prosperity while he sits idly at home; he cannot pray for health if his actions run counter to standard rules of hygiene. He cannot pray for wisdom if his mind is not prepared to receive wisdom. Everything depends on God's basic commitment: 'The Lord your God will bless you in all your work and in everything you put your hand to' (Deuteronomy 15:10)."[17]

We may understand from Rabbi HaLevy's words that God's blessing is with us at all times, it pours out upon the earth, it spreads over all of us.

---

17. Hayim David HaLevy, *Aseh Lecha Rav* (Tel Aviv: Society for the Publication of the Writings of HaRav Hayim David HaLevy, 1986), vol. 2, question 22.

Goodness is ever-present in our lives; prayer serves to raise our awareness of this ever-flowing compassion. Prayer does not change God's will – it changes us.

So, when we pray for a miracle, we are not actually asking God to intervene and overstep the boundaries He established for Himself from the time of creation. Of course doing so is well within God's abilities, but is beyond the usual terms of engagement that He established with us and that He would normally prefer to honor.

Actually, we are praying for God's help in encouraging a first-order miracle.

- We are asking Him to strengthen the stamina that we already have.
- We are asking him to embolden the bravery of our would-be deliverers.
- We are asking him to clarify the thinking of those who stand to cure us.
- We are asking him to inspire the humanity of those who might otherwise destroy us.

All such events are truly miraculous events, answers to our heartfelt prayers.

We have established that God can and does intervene in our lives at all times, mostly via first-order miracles. We have also established that at times, under certain circumstances, God will breach the natural order, implementing even second-order miracles when He deems it absolutely necessary.

With a better definition of the multiple levels of miracles in our lives, we are now prepared to approach the really difficult question, the title of this chapter and of the whole book as well.

Where's My Miracle?

And so we must ask, if personalized first-order or even second-order miracles are possible, if God can make special exceptions in exceptional cases, then what about me – "Where's my miracle?"

TEXT
Miracles Happen for Those Who Deserve Them
Rav Papa said to Abaye, "What is the difference between the

former generation and us, such that miracles happened for them, and not for us?"… He replied, "The former generations sacrificed themselves for the sanctity of God's name; we do not sacrifice ourselves for the sanctity of God's name."[18]

Why aren't we privileged to experience powerful, public miracles like the ones described in the Torah? Why doesn't God extend His outstretched arm against our enemies, as He did in Egypt and Canaan? Why doesn't He intervene to stop terrorists, to heal the sick, to release the unjustly imprisoned? Can't God arrange for miracles that will answer the prayers of the righteous and be a constant proof of His existence for all to see?

According to this third-century distinguished Babylonian scholar, second-order divine intervention is only forthcoming for those who are especially deserving, those who are willing to sacrifice their own lives to honor the sanctity of God's name. (I am assuming here that Rav Papa is speaking of second-order miracles, as it would be difficult to believe that he didn't accept the notion that first-order miracles are ever-present in our lives.) The implication of this assessment, brought in the name of Abaye, is that miracles happen only for those who deserve them: miracles are based purely upon merit.

Rambam, as we pointed out in the previous chapter, taught that under ideal circumstances, everything that happens to a person is a manifestation of God's will.

However, as can be seen from the following source, Rambam himself understood that for most people this is not the case.

COUNTER-TEXT
Miracles Happen for Those Who Are Closely Connected to God

An extraordinary thought has occurred to me just now which will serve to dispel doubts and reveal divine secrets. We have already explained…that providence watches over everyone endowed with intellect, in proportion to the measure of his intellect. In this way, providence is at all times watching over an individual endowed with a perfect consciousness of God, whose intellect is never distracted from its occupation with God.

---

18. Babylonian Talmud, Berachot 20a.

On the other hand, an individual endowed with such a perfect consciousness, but whose thought is sometimes distracted from God, is watched over by providence only during the time when he thinks of God; providence departs from him during such times when he is preoccupied with something else…. Therefore, it seems to me that all prophets or outstanding and faultless people who suffered from the evils of this world experienced this evil during such a time of distraction, the greatness of the calamity being directly in proportion to the duration of the period of his distraction or to the baseness of the matter with which he was preoccupied.

If this is so, the great doubt that led the philosophers to deny that divine providence watches over all human beings and to suggest that they are equal to all other animals is dispelled. For their proof was the fact that outstanding and fine people experienced great misfortunes…. If a person's thought is free from distraction, if he is conscious of God, may He be exalted, in the right way and rejoices in his consciousness of Him, that individual will never suffer evil of any kind. For he is with God and God is with him. When, however, he is distracted from Him, may He be exalted, and is thus separated from God and God from him, he becomes, as a result of this, a target for every type of evil that may befall him.[19]

With these bold words, Rambam explained how it is that one can be a firm believer in personal divine providence, while at the same time accepting the fact that there are many things that happen to good people that are not the direct will of God. In other words, the reason that God may *not* perform a miracle to prevent an individual's misfortune is a consequence of the person's disconnection from God at that particular moment. Rambam indicated that the evils that befell even the most righteous of people were the result of this distance, this disengagement from God, even for a brief instant. Ralbag echoed Rambam's perspective on this matter, writing:

When it is appreciated that evils do not derive directly from God, may He be blessed, it can easily be demonstrated that it is false to

---

19. Rambam, *Guide for the Perplexed* III:51.

say that divine providence extends over all individual members of
the human species.... For if God requites every person according
to his actions, good or bad – i.e., rewards for good actions or
punishments for evil actions, which is the view of these people –
then evil would derive directly from God. However, evil does not
stem directly from God, and hence divine providence does not
extend over individual people....[20]

It seems to me that if this was the case for the prophets and the most
righteous, then most certainly it is pertinent to the common person whose
consciousness of God's involvement in life is often quite limited. For most
people, then, according to this approach, the absence of miracles in a
person's life is not based on issues related to our general worthiness, but
rather, based on our lapsed connection with God, a result of the day-to-
day distractions in our lives.

Rambam offers us a significant explanation for the absence of second-
order miracles in our lives. This next text offers a different approach to this
same question.

COUNTER-TEXT

Miracles Happen Only When Necessary

**Rabbi Shmuel ben Rabbi Yitzchak said, "Abraham would not
have been saved from the furnace of fire had it not been for
the merit of his future grandson, Jacob." A parable explains
this: Once a man was brought to be judged before the sultan,
who ruled that the man should be burned to death. However,
through astrology, it was revealed to the sultan that in the
future, this man, should he not be killed, would have a daughter
who would one day marry the king. The sultan said, "It is worth
saving this man's life for the daughter who will one day marry
the king!" So too, Abraham was judged to be burned to death
in Ur Kasdim, and when it was revealed before God that in the
future, Abraham would have a descendant Jacob, God said, "It
is worth saving Abraham in the merit of Jacob!"[21]**

This text is what we might call a midrash on a midrash. According to
midrashic literature, Abraham himself came to the realization that there

---

20. Levi ben Gershom, *The Wars of the Lord*, 170–71.
21. Genesis Rabbah 63:2.

must be an all-powerful, ever-present, yet intangible God in the world. Nimrod, king and self-proclaimed god of Babylonia, was threatened by Abraham's teachings and beliefs, and decided to challenge him: Abraham was told that he must choose between renouncing his belief in this omniscient, omnipotent, omnipresent God or be thrown into a fiery furnace where he would surely meet an agonizing death. Abraham would not budge from his faith in God. He was thrown into the fiery furnace, and after three days and three nights in the furnace, he emerged unscathed.

The counter-text above, a midrashic elaboration on the story, presents a thought-provoking, even radical insight into the story. According to Rabbi Shmuel ben Yitzchak, a fourth-century Babylonian sage, although Abraham was of perfect faith, was generous, just, and faithful, nonetheless, these qualities did not bring about his miraculous deliverance. He was saved from his fiery fate because his grandson, Jacob, was destined to emerge from him.

In other words, it wasn't *merit* that drove God to intervene, to suspend nature for three days in order to save Abraham's life, not to mention God's good name. No, it was *necessity* that brought about this miracle. According to this approach, Abraham, with all of his merits, with all of his faith, would nonetheless have suffered and died in that inferno if it were not for the fact that God *needed* Jacob to be born into this world.

COUNTER-TEXT
Exodus from Egypt

The Holy One, blessed be He, only promised Abraham that He would take Israel out of the Egyptian exile, and not out from under the oppressive servitude that came in its wake. For it is certain that when Israel were in Egypt, they contaminated and polluted themselves with all types of impurity, until they found themselves at the forty-ninth [next to last] level of impurity, and the Holy One, blessed be He, saved them from falling into further contamination.[22]

This mystical text addresses the question of why it took so long for God to come along and redeem the Jewish people from Egypt. They had suffered for many, many years under their burdens and oppressive slavery. While

---

22. Zohar HaChadash, beginning of Parashat Yitro, 3b; http://www.israel613.com/books/ ZOHAR_CHADASH_YITRO.pdf.

the Torah indicates that it was after God heard their crying out to Him that He remembered His covenant with Abraham and began the process of redeeming them (Exodus 2:24), this text retells the story somewhat differently. Here, the sages remind us that that the actual promise to Abraham was that the nation would be redeemed from their exile after four hundred years – not that God would save them from their oppression (see Genesis 15:13). What then caused God to bring the exile in Egypt to an early conclusion, after only 210 years? The people were in a desperate situation. They had sunken so morally and spiritually low that God could wait no longer. The exodus with all of its wonders and miracles had to be put in place in order to save the nation from complete ruin – it was not an issue of worthiness, but a matter of dire necessity.

In 1999, I was living in Overland Park, Kansas. One day, the local newspaper carried a front-page story with the headline "A Day at a Time, A Step at a Time, A Smile at a Time."[23] The article was about Amber Ramirez, a fifteen-year-old girl from Lincoln, Nebraska, who suffered from a rare brain disease that caused hourly seizures and was slowly causing her to deteriorate. The only treatment possible was to surgically remove half of her brain in a procedure known as a hemispherectomy. The operation offered hope, but it would leave her with many physical and mental challenges. She faced the possibility of never understanding a written word, ever again. Amber befriended another teenage girl, Kacie Caves, from Tulsa, Oklahoma, who had undergone the same surgery at an earlier time. The paper reported words of encouragement that Kacie's mother, Regina Caves, shared with the Ramirez family. She said:

> I believe that God knows who to let this happen to. A lot of people couldn't handle it at all. We learned that we could.[24]

At the time, more than sixteen years had passed since the death of my mother. And here, in the words of a woman who lived day-to-day, face-to-face with her daughter's suffering, I found the simple, insightful understanding for which I had been searching for so many years.

In these few words, Regina Caves shared two very significant insights that must be considered when dealing with the question "Where's my miracle?"

---

23. *Kansas City Star*, September 18, 1999.
24. Ibid.

Insight #1: In most cases, God does not cause suffering, God does not send suffering, God does not desire suffering. Rather, when suffering happens, it's because God "lets it happen."

Insight #2: When we suffer, it's a sign that God knows that we have the ability to handle it.

Let me make something clear. I understand that these words are not necessarily comforting to the sufferer or the bereaved, especially at the time when the wound is fresh, when the loss is recent. I wholly subscribe to the sagacious advice of the second-century sage of the Land of Israel, Rabbi Shimon ben Elazar, who said: "Do not offer comfort when one's dead lies before him."[25] A bereaved parent, Harriet Sarnoff Schiff, recalls in a book she wrote about the tragic death of her young son that her clergyman, in an attempt to comfort her for her loss, took her aside and said, "I know that this is a painful time for you. But I know that you will get through it all right, because God never sends us more of a burden than we can bear. God only let this happen to you because he knows that you're strong enough to handle it." The author, mother of the deceased, remembers thinking, "If only I were a weaker person, Robbie would still be alive."[26]

I do not present this suggestion as a source of acute comfort, something I would necessarily share with a mourner at the peak of their mourning. But it appears to me that this approach is deserving of greater consideration as a means of coming to terms with God's role in human suffering.

My parents divorced when I was quite young. My father died in 1979. It was my mother who had raised me on her own. When I think back upon my mother's death in 1983, when I was only twenty, I recall my initial longings for a miracle, my sense that God was letting me down. How could God do this to me?

Deciding ultimately that it wasn't a punishment, neither for her nor for me, her only child, I was still left wondering why there was no miracle. What, after all, is the criterion for being eligible for a miracle? Was she really not deserving of a miracle? Had my mother not suffered enough in a challenging marriage that led to divorce? Did that suffering not make her presently eligible for a miracle? Was not the prospect of averting the pain that my poor grandmother was destined to feel every day for the next three

25. Mishnah Avot 4:18.
26. Cited in Harold Kushner, *When Bad Things Happen*, 26.

years that remained of her life enough reason to send a miracle at that time? And what about me? Was not my decision at age fourteen to become a fully observant Jew enough of a reason to bless me with a miracle?

But now I understand, and it makes so much sense.

Miracles, particularly second-order medical miracles, the kind that interfere with nature's course, the kind that leave doctors clueless, are not normally forthcoming. Although God is constantly responsible for facilitating first-order miracles, second-order supernatural interventions are less likely when He knows that we have the strength to handle the consequences.

As taught in the above midrash about Abraham, the criterion God has set for miraculous intervention in our individual lives is not based upon *merit*; rather, it is based upon *necessity*.

Let me repeat. *Miracles in our personal lives are not necessarily related directly to issues of reward and punishment.* This means that in many instances, *deserving* individuals will not experience miracles, simply because the situation does not require God's intervention. And in other instances, *undeserving* individuals may actually benefit from God's miraculous intervention, because God knows that they or their family or the world at large cannot handle the alternative!

This then serves as an alternative explanation for why we find suffering among the righteous and good things coming to the wicked. Theodicy becomes a problem when we assume that good and bad tidings are directly related to merit, rather than long-term issues of necessity.

From a human perspective, this doesn't seem fair. Why shouldn't God intervene to reward the righteous, and punish, or at the very least disassociate Himself, from the lot of the wicked? While this perspective seems logical, I believe that it represents a serious misunderstanding about the role of miracles in our lives.

Miracles by Necessity

On an individual level, miracles are not rewards for good behavior. Miracles are, rather, necessary measures that God must take, at times, despite His preference not to do so. (I realize that the Torah in many places seems to indicate that God will intervene in supernatural, miraculous ways for the Jewish people when they are following His commandments. When it comes to our national existence, it may very well be based in the long run upon a system of reward and punishment. It is for this reason that I am specifically referring here to miracles on the individual level.)

In April of 1999, a fifty-four-year-old woman, a member of our community, who had been in remission from breast cancer for around ten years, suffered a very serious relapse and passed away. At the time of her first bout with the disease, she and her husband, parents of three young children at the time, ages eight to twelve, were hospitalized simultaneously. Her husband too suffered from a life-threatening ailment. Her husband died, and she, as it was described to me, "made a miraculous recovery." She came out of the hospital and returned to a normal, active life. Ten or so years later, when she had the relapse, her youngest son had graduated high school. After the funeral I sat with the three siblings, who were in search of understanding. Were there no miracles to be found that could have spared the three of them from becoming orphans, bereft of both parents at such a young age?

I suggested to them that perhaps there had been a miracle. Perhaps ten years earlier, when the need was desperate, God had intervened and provided their mother with a second-order miracle, so that she could be there for them during their childhood, for God recognized that as a necessity. This time around, however, the situation was different.

To be absolutely clear, I did not propose that God sent the relapse; rather, I suggested that God knew that this time it was *not necessary to intervene*. The children, now all of them young adults, had been blessed with what they needed in life to get them through. God knew that they would be all right, that this time around they were prepared to handle the tragic situation, and, as always, God's preference was not to intervene through implementation of supernatural miracles. Not based upon merit, but rather, based upon necessity.

Let me state this clearly: I believe that when God chooses not to intervene, not to prevent an illness, not to head off an accident, or not to save a life, this too is meaningful. And not because God has willed it to happen.

It is meaningful because it teaches us that the miracle is not a necessity. It is a message to us that we, the human partners in this partnership, have *the capacity to deal with the ensuing results*. God will *only* intervene and make a "miracle" when He knows that it's beyond our personal or national capacity to cope with the natural consequences.

This approach has been a great inspiration to me in my life, and it is a perspective that I have had the opportunity to share with others, looking back on tragedy, in search of understanding. It has enabled me to review the events of my life and recognize that the sum total of my life experiences by the age of twenty had prepared me for the loss of my mother, and that the absence of a miracle at that time was not indicative of unworthiness, nor of any impotence on God's part. In the words of the Talmud, there were no miracles for us, because in most cases, *the world pursues its natural course.*[27] Neither my mother nor I were being punished or neglected by God. Rather, these experiences indicated that I was prepared to deal with the new circumstances that lay before me.

With hindsight, I can see that this most certainly was the case.

The Book of Job: More Questions Than Answers

When issues related to the encounter with suffering surface, it is rabbinic practice to straightaway reference the Book of Job. Job suffered the deaths of his seven sons and three daughters, as well as the loss of most of his worldly possessions. Essentially, he lost nearly everything that was important to him in his life. It is usually suggested that the story of Job's suffering ultimately serves to remind us that when faced with suffering and misfortune, we can never hope to comprehend the reasons for our misfortune. Only God knows why we suffer.

However, the ultimate message of the book is not so clear.

The problem with looking to Job for inspiration is that we, the readers, have access to information that Job does not. As the opening dialogues of the book indicate, Job's faith in God is being tested. God has authorized the terror and devastation that Job has suffered. Although God speaks to him via a powerful speech at the end of the book, He never tells Job what his suffering was really all about. Essentially, Job never knows what we know.

I have always wondered how Job would have reacted had he been told the plain truth. What would have happened if God had told Job that his entire life had been destroyed as a test of his faith? Would that have really comforted Job?

That's right, Job. I took the lives of your seven sons and three daughters, destroyed your home, your cattle, your servants, and your many possessions,

---

27. Babylonian Talmud, Avodah Zarah 54b.

plagued you with a painful skin disease, and have in general made your life miserable as a test, to find out if you really are my faithful servant, Job.

What actually provides Job with comfort at the end of the book is that God convinces him, through a very long monologue, that there is a divine purpose to everything, even if we can never hope to comprehend it. Would Job have been comforted if he knew the truth, if he found out that the divine purpose in his case was nothing more than an elaborate trial, meant to verify his loyalty?

There is something about the usual way we understand the Book of Job that is unsettling, that just doesn't make sense in terms of its internal narrative.

Additionally, as I wrote at the outset of this book, the whole premise that suffering is always the will of God has never served as an inspiration for me. The Book of Job, as normally understood, tells the story of suffering that is sent by God (or perhaps better said, authorized by God and sent by Satan, God's emissary) and asks that we take comfort in the knowledge that although we cannot comprehend it, there is always a purpose to our suffering.

However, if, as I have here suggested, suffering is alternatively understood to be the consequences of God's intentional decision not to get involved, of God's preference to abstain from direct intervention into the course of nature whenever possible, honoring His role and the role that we who are created in His image chose for ourselves from the beginning of time, then the image of Job being rigorously tested through suffering is most certainly not a model from which I can derive genuine personal inspiration.

Searching the text more closely, I believe I have found a fundamentally different understanding of the narrative of the story; an alternative reading that makes the story of Job's suffering more palatable, and God's role in that suffering more benign.

Chapter 8

JOB'S MISUNDERSTANDING

Why I Will Never Forget David Chatuel

During the bloodiest months of the Intifada, barely a week passed that from my living room I did not hear a bomb explode. The front of the war that was being waged against the Israeli people was not in distant Lebanon, or Syria, or along the Jordanian border. The front was located in the bus my husband rode to work, in the market where I did my Shabbat shopping, and at the neighborhood playground where I spent my afternoons watching my young daughters swing and slide and play.

Throughout those scary years, every time I had to exit the front door of our apartment in downtown Jerusalem, I felt as paralyzed with fear as a person forced at gunpoint to walk blindfolded through a minefield.

But the terror attack that hit closest to home did not take place in Jerusalem at all. The attack took place on May 2, 2004 when an Arab approached the car of Tali Chatuel and shot her and her four young daughters, point blank, twice in the head, and then riddled their bodies with dozens of bullets.

In one moment, David Chatuel, an idealistic elementary school principal and devoted father and husband, was left bereft of his whole family, his 34-year-old wife Tali Chatuel who was in her eighth month of pregnancy with the couple's first son, and his daughters Hila, 11, Hadar, 9, Roni, 7, and Meirav, 2. In one moment, everything had been taken from him, except the impossible and terrible wish that it could have been him instead of them.

For weeks following the attack, the image of this beautiful mother, a social worker who worked to rehabilitate terror victims, and her smiling, innocent daughters hung over me day after day. I could not help but remember that Tali Chatuel was only a few months older than me. I couldn't forget that those little girls were almost the same ages and bore such similar names to my own three daughters. I would go to sleep and see their faces, and wake up and see David Chatuel sobbing with his head in his hands at their funeral.

Over and over, I thought of this broken man's words mixed with the weeping of the thousands of mourners at the funeral for his wife and daughters, "Tali and my girls, I will never forget you until the day I die. I love you so much. I am left alone. My family has been taken from me. If even one of you was still alive..."

Throughout the four years of Intifada that left over a thousand Jews murdered, I had never felt so hopeless, so destroyed. How could I have any hope left when I saw this father weeping like a *modern-day Job* for his murdered family? How could I have any hope left when we were facing such a cruel and seemingly unstoppable enemy?[1]

Finding inspiration in the Book of Job is not a simple task. I suppose that considering David Chatuel a "modern-day Job" is meant to only put his loss into context. Like Job, in a matter of moments, his entire world had crumbled before his eyes. No one could explain to him why this happened: why to him, why to them, why at all?

I want to ask another question.

What is the ultimate message of the Book of Job? Is it a message of comfort? Is it a message of understanding? Does it help to explain our sufferings in this world, or does it simply exacerbate the dilemma?

Did Job Ever Exist?

Before we attempt to understand the book's message, let us consider if we are learning a lesson from a real person's historical experience, or is it human experience that has led to the creation of the story?

---

1. Chana (Jenny) Weisberg, *Passover: Rising from the Ashes*, March 24, 2007; http://www.aish.com/jewishissues/israeldiary/Passover_Rising_from_the_Ashes.asp. Reprinted with permission from Aish.com, a leading Judaism website. Italics mine.

TEXT
Advisor to Pharaoh

Rabbi Chiya ben Abba said in the name of Rav Simai: There were three in that plan to subdue the Jewish people in Egypt. They were Balaam, Job, and Jethro. Balaam, who devised it, was slain; Job, who silently acquiesced, was afflicted with sufferings; Jethro, who fled, merited that his descendants should sit in the Chamber of Hewn Stone.[2]

According to this text, the rabbis of the Talmud suggest that Job was a real person, who lived during the time of our slavery in Egypt and functioned as an advisor to Pharaoh. When the plan to drown the newborn Jewish boys in the Nile was conceived by Balaam, another advisor to Pharaoh, Job neglected to speak out against the plan, and so, argue the sages here, for this he suffered. Another Talmudic text also argues that Job was a real person, but the rabbis quoted there offer a whole variety of options as to exactly when he lived.[3]

It is interesting to read this and other rabbinic and contemporary texts that search to justify Job's suffering. After all, those familiar with the story know that the narrative itself seems to indicate that there is no humanly perceivable explanation for Job's suffering. Only God knows the reason. Rabbi Joseph B. Soloveitchik, for instance, suggested that Job was guilty of not using the blessings that were his to accelerate historical events, to relieve the burdens carried by the great heroes of the ages. "God addressed himself to Job though abundance and wealth, through the ecstasy of joy. Job missed the message. The pendulum swung toward the catastrophic revelation...."[4]

Although there are those who believed Job to have been a real person, a separate opinion cited in the Talmud suggests otherwise, that the story of Job is just that – a story – and its message is the thoughts of one author attempting to deal with the eternal questions associated with the suffering of the righteous.

---

2. Bablyonian Talmud, Sotah 11a.
3. Babylonian Talmud, Baba Batra 15a–b.
4. Joseph B. Soloveitchik, *Out of the Whirlwind, Essays on Mourning, Suffering and the Human Condition*, ed. David Shatz (New York: Ktav Publishing House, 2002), 139.

COUNTER-TEXT
A Fictional Character
**A certain rabbi was sitting before Rabbi Shmuel bar Nachmani
and in the course of his expositions remarked, "Job never was
and never existed, but is only an archetypal figure."**[5]

Rabbi Shmuel bar Nachmani was a fourth-century scholar of the Land
of Israel. The implication of this Talmudic position is that the story of
Job is a fictional story created in order to present a religious response to
the challenges of theodicy. When we read the story, we recognize it as
representative of one Jewish approach, rather than *the* Jewish approach
to suffering.

Either way, ostensibly the book presents us with an upright man who
has been blessed with good fortune and plenty. He is described as "perfect
and upright, one who feared God and turned away from evil."[6]

I wish to take a closer look at the story of Job, for, in my opinion,
without some innovative interpretation, the story presents us with religious
challenges that go beyond the suffering of the righteous, challenges that
typically go unaddressed.

Job Revisited

Opening the Book of Job, we have barely met the main character when
the narrative suddenly shifts to some sort of celestial convention. At this
gathering of angels, God brings the loyalty of his devout servant, Job, to
the attention of one of the other attendees, the adversarial angel named
Satan. Apparently it is within Satan's job description to test the faith of
the righteous. Satan voices his suspicions of Job's authenticity, and God
acknowledges that one might mistakenly assume that Job's faith is only a
result of his good fortune. Thereafter, God gives Satan the "green light" to
test Job's faith.

At first, Job is tested through the "repossession" of all of his wealth,
followed by the tragic deaths of all of his children, his seven sons and three
daughters. The words uttered by Job when faced with these unspeakable
misfortunes clearly sum up what for many is considered to be the take-

---

5. Babylonian Talmud, Baba Batra 15a.
6. Job 1:1.

away message of the whole book: "The Lord has given, and the Lord has taken away, blessed be the name of the Lord."[7]

When, nonetheless, Job spouts forth with this well-known declaration of faith, God allows for him to be further afflicted, this time with an unbearably painful skin disease. His life seems worthless; his own wife tells him to get it over with, "Do you yet have integrity? Curse God, and die!"[8] she says. But, again, in righteous fashion, Job responds to her frustration with words that stand for a faith that could not be budged: "What? Shall we accept only the good at the hand of God, and not accept the bad?"[9] Still, Job professes his unwavering faith in God.

The bulk of the remaining story is made up of the dialogues between Job and his friends, who attempt to bring comfort by proffering various suggestions as to the justice of his predicament, asserting that there is always a good reason for our sufferings. Job, however, refuses to accept any of their suggestions. He can accept that God is all-powerful, and that God can do as God pleases; however, he can think of no logical justification for his suffering. Tensions rise, as each of the friends gets more and more frustrated with Job's refusal to accept that his suffering is somehow deserved.

Although Job righteously stated from the outset that God has the right to take away blessing and substitute it with curse, he nonetheless refuses to accept that he is in any way deserving of God's severe decree upon him and his family.

If that's the case, then what *is* the explanation for Job's suffering?

Rabbi Harold Kushner devotes a chapter of his popular book to the story of Job. For Kushner, the author of the Book of Job is taking a radical position, a position that Kushner himself adopts: that while both God and Job are good, the problem is that God is really not all-powerful. That is why Job suffers, because God cannot do anything about it.

However, the simple understanding of the ending of the book is that Job seems to clearly reject this conclusion. For as soon as Job makes the statement, "I know that You can do everything,"[10] admitting that God is all-powerful and that he has been out of place in his comments about God,

---

7. Job 1:21.
8. Job 2:9.
9. Job 2:10.
10. Job 42:2.

God blesses him with fortune and children, giving him "twice as much as he had before."

This seems to make it clear that the author of the book acknowledged God as all-powerful, able to return to Job all that he had lost. In fact, from the very beginning of the book, God is calling the shots.

An Alternative Explanation

What then might be another way to explain Job's suffering? I believe that the key is to be found in Job's final words at the end of the book.

The grand finale of the story, introduced by God's direct, "out of the whirlwind" communication with Job, leaves Job speechless.

> Then the Lord answered Job out of the whirlwind, and said:
> Who is this that darkens counsel through words, without knowledge?
> Gird up now your loins like a man;
> for I will demand of you, and declare you unto Me.
> Where were you when I laid the foundations of the earth?
> Answer Me, if you have the understanding.[11]

In acknowledgment of his mistake, Job responds,

> What shall I answer you? I lay my hand upon my mouth.[12]

What mistake was Job acknowledging?

We are led to believe that God has silenced Job's elaborate complaints, his demand for justice and understanding. We are led to believe that God has rebuked Job for implying that his sufferings were without cause, that they were undeserved. Job must now acknowledge that he cannot understand God's ways, for no mortal can hope to fathom the depths of God's conduct.

The problem with this traditional analysis of the story, as I see it, is that it ignores the elephant in the middle of the room.

Let's go back. As the story opens, we are told that Job was most certainly righteous, a devout servant of God. He by no means deserves to

---

11. Job 38:1–4.
12. Job 40:4.

suffer. In essence, his rejection of any notion of justice in his sufferings is very much in place. God had no just reason to cause him such suffering.

The end of our story seems to have forgotten all about this opening to the story, directing us to emulate Job who has admitted that he was mistaken.

But he wasn't mistaken! Was he?

As the tale comes to a close, the author seems to have completely forgotten this significant detail of the story! The author's apparent disregard of the opening passages of the story, where we learned that this was all about testing the faithful Job, makes it very difficult for me to be open to any lessons at the end of the story. Why should Job admit that his suffering must have meaning beyond his comprehension when we have been informed by the narrator of the story that it was really all just one big test?

For this reason, I suggest the following rereading of the story, which has helped me not only to understand the story better, but to find inspiration in it as well.

Job was a righteous person, a faithful believer, a God-fearing individual. He felt blessed in his life; he took nothing for granted. However, one day, at a certain point in his life, things began changing. His life began to crumble all around him. Crime, war, negligence, and natural forces took from him all that he had valued in his life. It *seemed* to Job that he was being tested, that his faith was under scrutiny. Faced with these tragedies, he was determined to pass the tests. He uttered words that he thought to be most suitable on such occasions. He attributed his losses to God's decision to take away from Job everything that He had given to him, in order to test the true strength of his convictions.

I am suggesting here that the celestial conventions at the beginning of the story are not meant to be understood as actual occurrences, but rather, the author provides them as imaginary metaphors for what Job, the sufferer, was feeling.[13] Job was feeling tested, and so he read his own predicament in a devout religious fashion, declaring that everything that happens to us in this world is by the word of God.

---

13. In his *Guide for the Perplexed* (II:42), Maimonides explains that any story in Tanach that involves angels never actually occurred, was no more than a dream. According to my reading, Job's interpretation of his suffering appears before the description of the actual tragedies; I contend that this is a literary tool meant to reflect the chronology of events as understood by Job.

This all-encompassing statement by Job, I might argue, is Job's tragic flaw, the fundamental mistake for which he is rebuked at the end of the book.

Let me explain.

Job's Misunderstanding

Job's declaration – "The Lord has given, and the Lord has taken away, blessed be the name of the Lord"[14] – asserts that everything that happens in this world, for good and for bad, emanates originally from God. This assertion brings along with it the corollary that everything that happens must happen for a reason. In other words, if everything emanates from God, and God is just, then all suffering must happen for good reason. When Job's three friends preach this message during their visits, they are essentially just reinforcing that which Job himself had been maintaining. *If everything is from God, and God is just, then everything that happens must be justified – especially suffering.*

> And Job again took up his parable, and said:
>
> Oh that I were as in the months of old,
> as in the days when God watched over me;
>
> When His lamp shined above my head,
> and by His light I walked through darkness;
>
> As I was in the days of my youth,
> when the council of God was upon my tent;
>
> When the Almighty was yet with me,
> and my children were about me.[15]

For the bulk of the Book of Job, we encounter an individual who has been caught in the midst of this great quandary, this inescapable dilemma, the very dilemma that has preoccupied human beings since ancient times.

God has abandoned him, turned his back upon him, causing him to suffer.

I suggest, therefore, that when God appeared and spoke with Job "out of the whirlwind," He came to outline the complexity of existence, the

---

14. Job 1:21.
15. Job 29:1–5.

intricate interconnectedness of all life forms, for the specific purpose of highlighting Job's fundamental misunderstanding: his belief that everything that happens to us is God's express will, rather than the result of a complex web of cause-and-effect relationships built into the fabric of existence.

Job's theology was too simplistic. That was his mistake. Bad can happen for all sorts of reasons; not specifically because God has so decreed it.

In a sense, Job brought the arguments of his companions upon himself. And now, realizing the folly of his simplistic analysis of life's ups and downs, he stands silent before God. Job's very own declarations of faith in the face of suffering, of God's hand in taking away blessing and in sending forth evil, are actually what lead his friends to conjecture that there must be a cause for his suffering. In other words, if this suffering was sent via God, as Job professed over and over, then how can it be without purpose?

What leads Job to become more and more frustrated throughout the book, following each subsequent interchange with his colleagues, is that they are pressing him to accept the logical conclusion of his own premise. If Job accepts that his suffering comes from God, then he is obliged to find meaning in that suffering. About this they are absolutely right!

The point of the book is that Job's assumptions from the very beginning are ultimately the cause of his great distress. The desire to force things to make sense, to assume that everything is from God and that everything is purposeful – this is what leads to Job's great frustration.

When God appears to Job "out of the whirlwind," He shares no great insights that help to explain the logic of what has happened to Job. And yet, for Job, the message of the "whirlwind speech" is clear:

1. I know that You can do everything, that nothing stands in your way.

2. I mistakenly declared that my suffering was Your doing – I can no longer say that I know that for sure, for I now realize there is so much I do not know.

3. I am remorseful for the ill-will that I have caused.

These, I suggest, are the essential lessons that Job learns and acknowledges, as he responds to God's powerful revelation with the words "What shall I answer you? I lay my hand upon my mouth."[16]

---

16. Job 40:4.

Immediately after Job makes this confession, God's wrath turns upon Job's colleagues. "For you have not spoken appropriately about Me, as has Job." In other words, once Job understood that the suffering he had experienced was not sent by God, neither as a test, nor as punishment, so too must all of his friends accept this truth and begin to speak differently! And so, they were instructed to undo the damage they had caused. They were required to do two things: they must first ask forgiveness from Job, and then they were to bring burnt offerings before God. That is to say, first Job had to forgive them for all of their incitement, and then God too would be willing to forgive them. They did as God instructed them, Job prayed that they be forgiven, and so they were.

Things began to change for Job; his fortunes returned. Seeing this, family and friends re-approached him. They too were curious to understand the nature of this turnaround. Only now, surrounded by evidence of a reversal in his fortune, people were ready to listen intently, to empathize with him and comfort him on his great suffering. However, since they were not a part of the developing story and had not heard the word of God nor contemplated all that Job had, we meet them as they continue to display the common religious understandings that Job had formerly bought into as well, as they proceed to share their condolences and attempt to comfort him for "all of the evil that God had brought upon him."[17] This element of the narrative serves as a reminder to us that without the critical insights offered by this story, people of faith will always make the same assumptions that Job had made throughout his life.

Job finally understood that God had neither abandoned him nor tested his faith. Job had imagined all of that, including the conversations between God and Satan, for the purpose of making some sense of his suffering.

For me, this is what makes the Book of Job so inspiring. This is the reason that it was made a part of the Bible – to teach us that while common religious belief is to assume that God is behind all suffering and evil, in reality, that is not usually the case. God is neither testing us, nor punishing us, nor sending us sufferings of love in order to reward us in our future life. Job and his friends thought this to be the case – however, they were all mistaken. There was no test, there was no punishment – there was only a very tragic concurrence of devastating events that added up to great suffering in the life of Job, a common man of faith.

---

17. Job 42:11.

In the epilogue to the story, as we are told of the rebuilding of Job's family and his wealth, we are not bearing witness to some rewards that Job earned through passing a test of his faith – after all, can ten dead children ever really be replaced with ten new ones?

God's blessings were not forthcoming in order to make up for what He had taken away. Rather, God blessed Job because God is benevolent, because God cares, because God loves Job. Job did not suffer as the result of some sick celestial wager, and in the end, he was not blessed as a result of some sort of compensation package from God for sufferings endured or faith professed.

As human beings, we often assume that the world revolves around us; Job learned that this is not always the case. Therefore, another element in understanding why it is that at times good people suffer and bad people prosper may include coming to some new realizations as to our place as human beings within God's vast plans for the universe.

Chapter 9

FOR WHAT PURPOSE
DID GOD CREATE MOSQUITOES?

What else do we learn from God's four-chapter-long rebuke of Job? Let's come back to this question after considering the following.

The complexity of the world in which we live is truly remarkable. When we begin to consider every last detail, in terms of function, size, shape, color, etc., we can't help but marvel at the details and wonder, "Why?" When my wife was studying to be a nurse, she was required to take a course in microbiology. She would often come home from class and remark, "It is impossible to study microbiology and not believe in God!"

Given the infinite number of elements that make up our world, from the microscopic to the mammoth, it is not surprising that Jewish scholars have brought up the question of "purpose" on many occasions. Is there really a unique purpose to everything God created in this world? And if so, can we ever fathom that purpose?

Everything and Its Purpose

One prevalent approach takes into consideration the question of why God created the things that seem so unnecessary in our world, such as fleas and mosquitoes. Couldn't we live without them?

TEXT
God's Agents
Even things which appear to be superfluous in the world, such as flies, fleas, and mosquitoes, they are also part of the creation of the world, and God performs His operations through the agency of all of them, even through a snake, mosquito, or frog.[1]

---

1. Genesis Rabbah 10:7.

Sometimes their purpose may be obvious. But even when no purpose is apparent to us, we can be sure that one nevertheless does exist. The snake did not just happen to come into existence; the mosquito did not just spontaneously appear. God intended for there to be such creatures in our world, and all of them serve as His agents for one purpose or another. Even if science never identifies their real purpose, even if they seem completely useless, our tradition tells us that everything has its purpose:

> Even things you see as superfluous [*meyutarin*] in this world – like flies, fleas, and mosquitoes – they are part of the greater scheme of the creation of the world, as it says, "And God saw all that He had created, and behold, it was very good" (Genesis 1:31).
>
> And Rabbi Acha bar Rabbi Chanina said, even things you see as superfluous in this world – like snakes and scorpions – they are part of the greater scheme of the creation of the world.[2]

Scientists have explained that houseflies belong to a group of flies called "filth flies." Filth flies, also known as saprophytes, get their names because they are important for breaking down decaying material. Young flies digest dead trees, dead animals, and even animal wastes, creating necessary topsoil for plants to grow in. Once a fly reaches its adult stage, it is important for providing food for insect-eating animals, such as frogs. Of course, then the purpose of frogs becomes evident: to keep the number of flying insects in check. And so on, and so forth…

Every aspect of creation, every detail of our world, is regarded with great respect and reverence. Our responsibility to guard the world, as commanded to Adam and Eve in the Garden of Eden, makes it incumbent upon us to preserve every element of the natural world in which we live.

Created for Whom?

However, even given our fundamental belief in the purpose of all of creation, the bigger question still remains: for whose benefit were all of these detailed creations brought into existence?

Think of it this way: When I was growing up, I loved to go swimming. Given the choice of swimming in a pool or swimming in a lake, I could never decide which I preferred. Both a swimming pool as well as a lake

---

2. Exodus Rabbah 10:1.

served the purpose of providing a place to cool down on those hot summer days; both were sources of recreation to enjoy with friends. However, while it is clear that this is the purpose of a swimming pool, can we definitely say that swimming is the purpose of a crystal-clear lake tucked away amid a cluster of lofty, tree-covered mountains?

Is that the reason that God created lakes? Or do lakes exist mainly for environmental purposes, with recreational swimming being just a side benefit of that creation?

Among the sages of the Talmud, this was a matter of disagreement. One approach advocated by the rabbis teaches that all of God's creations were ultimately fashioned in service of humankind. Whether directly or indirectly, every detail of the creation was put into place in order to ensure the continued existence of the human race, the culmination of all of God's creative endeavors.

TEXT
Genesis – A Human-Centered World
Rav Yehudah said in Rav's name: Among all the things that God created in His universe, He created nothing that is useless. God created the snail as a cure for a wound, the fly as a cure for the sting of the wasp, the gnat as a cure for the bite of a serpent, the serpent as a cure for a sore, and the spider as a cure for the sting of a scorpion.[3]

Rav understood that everything God created was created for a purpose – a purpose that would serve the needs of humankind. Even those creatures that annoy us, or even threaten to cause us injury, creatures that we might prefer to live without – all of them exist to benefit humankind.

Throughout history, many have embraced this philosophy. For instance, the third-century scholar Rabbi Elazar proclaimed that the Holy One, blessed be He, says: "The whole world was created for humankind's sake alone."[4] Similarly, the Mishnah, codified at the end of the second century, teaches that God created every human using the stamp of the first human, and yet not one of them resembles another. Therefore, proclaim the rabbis

---

3. Babylonian Talmud, Shabbat 77b.
4. Babylonian Talmud, Berachot 6b.

of the Mishnah, "every single person is obliged to say: the world was created for my sake."[5]

This philosophy considers all of existence through the human lens, perceiving the existence of an unspoken chain of command that places human beings at the very top of creation. This being the case, then we can assume that everything that is less profound than the human being must have been placed in the universe to serve us.

However, such an approach brings with it some serious theological problems related to all that we have been considering throughout the book.

If humankind is the center of the universe, then why do so many bad things happen to us? Why are there earthquakes, hurricanes, tsunamis, volcanic eruptions, and other such natural disasters that kill large numbers of people? What about disease? What about genetic disorders? Assuming that everything is here to serve and benefit us, and that God is almighty, benevolent, and just, how do we explain the injustices?

Although the rabbis of the Talmud and midrash (second through sixth centuries) seem to generally line up in the direction of viewing humankind at the center, that did not stop Rambam (of the twelfth century) from thinking differently, thereby offering us the following alternate approach:

COUNTER-TEXT
Everything Exists for Its Own Sake

I consider therefore the following opinion as most correct according to the teaching of the Bible, and most in accordance with the results of philosophy; namely, that the universe does not exist for man's sake, but that each being exists for its own sake, and not because of some other thing. Thus we believe in the creation, and yet need not inquire as to what purpose is served by each existing species, because we assume that God created all parts of the universe by His will; some things for their own sake, and some for the sake of other beings, those other beings having been created for their own sake. In the same manner as it was the will of God that man should exist, so it was His will that the heavens with their stars should exist, that there should be angels, and each of these beings is itself the purpose of its own existence....

---

5. Mishnah Sanhedrin 4:5.

In other words, humankind is not the focus of all of creation. Rather, every aspect of creation was simply the manifestation of God's will. Period.

> **And when you study the book that leads all who want to be led to the truth, and is therefore called Torah (Guide), from the beginning of the account of the creation to its end, you will comprehend the position which we attempt here to expound. For no part of the creation is described as being in existence for the sake of another part, but each part is declared to be the product of God's will, and to satisfy by its existence the intention [of the Creator]. This is expressed by the phrase "And God saw that it was good" (Genesis 1:4). For you know that which we explained.... The Torah speaks in the language of human beings. And "good" is an expression we apply to that which conforms to its purpose.[6]**

According to Rambam, anthropocentrism (putting humankind at the middle of everything) is nothing more than wishful thinking. Humankind is just one of numerous organisms that exist within a single, complex ecosystem. We may have superior abilities, but from a religious perspective we are to view humankind as but one small part of a vast universe. God created this universe in all of its detail, and humankind is but one organism that is part of this immeasurable entity.

John Muir, an American philosopher of the nineteenth century, echoed this same idea. After illustrating the anthropocentric philosophy described above, he proceeds to critique it:

> But if we should ask these profound expositors of God's intentions [proponents of anthropocentrism], "How about those man-eating animals – lions, tigers, alligators – which smack their lips over raw man? Or about those myriads of noxious insects that destroy labor and drink his blood? Doubtless man was intended for food and drink for all these?" Oh, no! Not at all! These are unresolvable difficulties connected with Eden's apple and the Devil. "Why does water drown its lord? Why do so many minerals poison him? Why are so many plants and fishes deadly enemies? Why is the

---

6. Rambam, *Guide for the Perplexed* III:13.

lord of creation subjected to the same laws of life as his subjects?"
Oh, all these things are satanic, or in some way connected with
the first garden.

Now, it never seems to occur to these far-seeing teachers
that Nature's object in making animals and plants might possibly
be first of all the happiness of each one of them, not the creation
of all for the happiness of one. Why should man value himself
as more than a small part of the one great unit of creation? And
what creature of all that the Lord has taken the pains to make is
not essential to the completeness of that unit – the cosmos? The
universe would be incomplete without man; but it would also be
incomplete without the smallest trans-microscopic creature that
dwells beyond our self-centered eyes and knowledge.[7]

If this is the case, if humankind does not really sit at the center of the
universe, then perhaps the first and foremost priority for the universe as a
whole is to guarantee its own survival – with or without humankind.

Humankind has the ability and the privilege to actively partake in this
great system that we call nature. We have the choice to be productive and
cautious, thereby preserving ourselves and the balanced network in which
we function, or to be destructive and reckless, destroying that balance and
ourselves along with it.

In the 1960s, the independent research scientist Dr. James Lovelock
formulated a scientific hypothesis that suggests that all living creatures on
earth, from the tiniest of the bacteria to the largest of the mammals, are
contributing to maintaining an optimum environment for all of life. In other
words, the activities of all forms of life on earth are actually contributing at
all times to provide for earth's survival. The planet will regulate variables,
such as climate, to protect itself in order to ensure its own survival.

He called this idea the "Gaia Hypothesis." Again, it suggests we realize
that it is in fact the planet Earth itself that is at the center of existence, not
we human beings. In 2006, Lovelock wrote:

Our planet has kept itself healthy and fit for life, just like an
animal does, for most of the more than three billion years of its

---

7.   John Muir, "Cedar Keys," in *A Thousand-Mile Walk to the Gulf* (New York: Houghton
     Mifflin, 1916); http://www.yosemite.ca.us/john_muir_writings/a_thousand_mile_
     walk_to_the_gulf/chapter_6.html.

existence. It was ill luck that we started polluting at a time when the sun was too hot for comfort. We have given Gaia a fever and soon her condition will worsen to a state like a coma. She has been there before and recovered, but it took more than 100,000 years.

We will do our best to survive, but, sadly, I can't see the US or the emerging economies of China and India cutting back in time and they are the main source of emissions. The worst will happen and survivors will have to adapt to a hell of a climate.[8]

With these thoughts in mind, we are now ready to return to the "out of the whirlwind" speech, uttered by God in the wake of Job's protests. It seems that in the details of this powerful poetic monologue lies an eternal message that is generally overlooked.

Revisiting the Whirlwind

Reading a number of selections from the whirlwind speech, a common theme is repeated. God asks Job,

> Who cuts a path for the flood,
> Or a way for the lightning of the thunder,
>
> Causing it to rain on land where no man lives,
> On the wilderness, wherein there is no man?
>
> To satisfy the desolate wasteland
> To make the wilderness blossom
> And to cover it with grass?[9]

God reprimands Job for his protests by pointing out to him that it is He, God, Who looks after the needs of all of His creations, even those that have no relevance to human life. He makes sure that it rains in places where no human being will ever step foot. He concerns himself with the "desolate

---

8. James Lovelock, "The Earth Is About to Catch Morbid Fever That May Last 100,000 Years," the *Independent*, January 16, 2006; http://www.independent.co.uk/opinion/ commentators/james-lovelock-the-earth-is-about-to-catch-a-morbid-fever-that-may-last-as-long-as-100000-years-523161.html. Printed by permission of the author and the *Independent*.
9. Job 38:25–27.

wasteland," enabling the wilderness to bloom and turn green – even though such places are well outside the realm of human life. Job must realize that everything does not revolve solely around human life.

> Will you hunt the prey for the lioness?
> Or satisfy the appetite of the young lions,
>
> When they couch in their dens,
> And lie in wait in their lair?
>
> Who provides for the raven his prey,
> When his young ones cry unto God,
> And wander for lack of food?[10]

The goings-on of life in the animal kingdom are far beyond the usual realm of human interest. Yet the details of animal survival, from birth to death, are in the realm of God's concern. God here is making a powerful point to Job, reminding him that human life in general, and Job's life in particular, is only part of a much bigger picture. God shepherds the entire world along, providing for the overall thriving of all of life on the planet.

What happens when there are conflicting needs between, for example, an ocean's need to release heat and the needs of the human beings residing along the coast of Florida to live in safety?

A hurricane is nature's way of transferring heat from the hotter southern climates to the cooler northern climates when air in the south heats up too much. The ocean heats up in the summer because the earth is closer to the sun. A hurricane can start to form when the sun heats the water to at least 82 degrees Fahrenheit, and hot air and water vapor begin rising from the ocean at faster and faster rates until the air begins to circulate counterclockwise, forming stronger and stronger winds that whirl with increasing speed. The moist, hot winds of a hurricane swirl upward around a calm column of low-pressure air, which becomes the eye of the storm.

Nature sends the hurricanes northward to cooler climates by the steering currents, air circulating around high and low pressure systems. So, when the hurricane hits the coast of Florida, should those whose homes are destroyed need to believe that God is punishing them?

---

10. Ibid. 38:39–41.

God's speech to Job attempts to explain to him that God is obligated to preserve all of His creations, and not all that happens in the world is meant to be taken as a message to humankind.

> Will the wild ox consent to serve you,
> Or will he spend the night in your manger?

> Can you bind the wild ox in a furrow with ropes,
> Or will he harrow the valleys after you?

> Will you trust him, because his strength is great,
> Or will you leave your labor to him?

> Will you rely on him,
> That he will bring home your seed,
> And gather the corn of your threshing floor?[11]

Some of God's creations are completely unmatched for coexistence with human beings. They have no place within the realm of human life. The wild ox, for instance, is entirely unfit for domestication. This being the case, Job must realize that there are many dimensions of existence that not only do not provide for human life, but that can be detrimental and downright dangerous to human beings should they have cause to cross paths. The wild ox, with all of its strength, cannot be relied on to work on a farm. His immense strength cannot be harnessed. Yet, the wild ox does exist in the world, and human beings would be advised to keep their distance, when at all possible.

The wild ox, I would suggest, represents those powerful forces that exist in our world that are often unable to be controlled. When out of control, these forces will endanger human life. Bears, tigers, sharks – such ferocious animals have parallels in the bacterial world as well, where the spread of deadly bacterial infections on epidemic levels can and has at times decimated pockets of human life. These bacteria are not sent into the world like the Angel of Death to do God's bidding; rather, as the wild ox, they exist for their own sakes as part of the creation. However, if they do happen to come into contact with human life, then, like an encounter

---

11. Ibid. 39:9–12.

between a human being and the wild ox, the results can potentially be catastrophic.

> Does the eagle soar at your command
> and build his nest on high?
>
> He dwells on a cliff and stays there at night;
> a rocky crag is his stronghold.
>
> From there he seeks out his food;
> his eyes detect it from afar.
>
> His young ones feast on blood,
> and where the slain are, there is he.[12]

The mighty eagle is a sight to see. And yet, it is clear that the eagle and we inhabit very different parts of the earth. Nesting high on the cliffs, seeking shelter and protection from amid the cracks in the rocks, we stand in awe as the eagle flies above us; his world is so very different from our own.

And yet, when there are slain among us, when corpses lay on the battlefield in the aftermath of a war, or when bodies are washed up on the beach in the aftermath of a shipwreck, the eagle may be there, finding nourishment amid the human remains. The eagle will not mourn the death, but will instead find it useful in its own quest for survival.

Humanity must continue to exist, and the eagle must survive as well.

We live in parallel worlds, yet both of us are parts of God's creation. God reminds Job that the eagle is not sent forth by God to desecrate, to add insult to the tragic events; but rather, it comes forth for one reason alone: to provide for its own survival. Much of nature functions in the same way – at times seriously impinging upon humanity in an effort to provide for its own continuity.

What additional lesson, then, does the whirlwind speech come to teach us?

I would like to suggest that implicit in the story of Job, as I see it, is a new picture of our relationship to God and to nature. Human values, as I understand the whirlwind speech, are not written into the DNA of life. Justice should not be considered a law of nature in this world. Rather it is human nature – perhaps a condition for human dignity – that we

---

12. Ibid. 39:27–30.

love and seek justice. But it is naïve – even arrogant – to suppose that the universe conforms to our human sense of justice. Perhaps this arrogance is one source of the sometimes-angry tone of God's voice from the whirlwind.

Admittedly, such a vision is unusual in Judaism. The more common anthropocentric picture is so strong in Jewish tradition that one usually thinks of the ideas that I have here suggested as not only outside of Judaism, but as bordering on heretical.

However, this understanding of the whirlwind speech offers us another way of contending with what we perceive as the unjust suffering of the innocent – not by denying the reality of the injustice, but by relinquishing the unreasonable expectation that the universe, with its multiple agendas, can still be ethically consistent according to human assessments.

Now, the price we pay for accepting this approach is that we complicate the direct correlation between God's goodness and love for justice on the one side, with the ethical unity of the world around us and all that happens in it on the other. (Not that the association was ever simple!) We no longer need to profess our faith in a world where all that happens is just; rather, we can choose to believe in justice as an ideal that we are committed to, in partnership with God.

Suffering remains, as it must, a serious human problem. But perhaps this partial glimpse at things from God's perspective can help us to cope. Realizing that at times what's best for human beings and what's best for other elements of God's creation may not be in tandem, we can begin to come to terms with the resulting toll of human suffering at the hands of nature, understanding it as an unfortunate conflict of interests rather than a divine mandate.

Chapter 10

MULTIPLE TRADITIONS:
HOW DO I CHOOSE WHAT TO BELIEVE?

The way of belief I have chosen,
Your judgments have I lain before me....
(Psalms 119:30)

Feeling confused?

I have presented you, the reader, with a lot of information. In many cases, the texts I have included have been in direct conflict with one another, presenting you with incompatible traditions. What will you do with all of this? How will you choose what to believe?

At the conclusion of an adult-education lesson that I was teaching on the subject of chapter 4, "Do People Die Before Their Time?" we had just read the text describing the Angel of Death's mix-up, having taken the wrong Miriam, Miriam the caregiver instead of Miriam the hairdresser. Essentially, the text was describing what amounted to a tragic premature death-by-accident that was clearly not a part of some unknown divine plan.

One student, a woman in her fifties, blurted out, "That's more comforting than anything else we have learned 'til now!"

I looked at the rest of the class. Some were shaking their heads up and down, others from side-to-side. The ensuing discussion confirmed that different traditions speak to different people, and that we are fortunate that the sages left us this variety of legitimate approaches.

Our textual tradition has preserved for us multiple approaches to the difficult questions associated with the suffering of the innocent, the seeming injustices that are part of human existence. Each position serves to answer certain questions, and at the same time raises others.

- How will you deal with conflicting texts like the ones we
  have encountered throughout this book?

- How will you choose which approach is right?

- What should you choose to believe?

As usual, there are differing opinions about this as well.

Conflicting Opinions about Conflicting Texts

There are those who, when confronted with texts in conflict, will search
for ways to resolve the conflict, to eliminate the contradiction. They will
diligently search for ways to reinterpret certain texts that seem to be in
complete opposition to other texts, with the conviction that it is only in
the resolution of the conflict that the truth is to be uncovered.

TEXT
Conflicting Texts Offer Opportunities to Uncover Truth
**It is well known that an argument involving contradictory
positions in analysis and study causes a matter to come to
light, and the truth to become known and clarified, free of
any doubt whatsoever. Therefore, doubts, comments, and
objections lead the way to the attainment of the desired goal.
The philosopher himself [Aristotle] said that doubts make
people wise. It is fitting for anyone seeking knowledge of the
truth in every book and branch of wisdom to keep this idea
in mind. It is known that doubts will not be resolved unless
there are opposing opinions, asking and answering, so that the
matter will come to light.[1]**

According to this approach, the process of investigation and discovery that
arises in the wake of encountering conflicting perspectives enables us to
ultimately arrive at the true understanding of that issue. Even the doubts
and confusion that we may experience along the way will, upon further
consideration, serve to strengthen our grasp of the subject, and clarify the
details more precisely.

---

1. Lev Avot, Avot 5:17, a commentary on Tractate Avot written by Shmuel di Ozeda, a
    disciple of the Ari, *z"l*.

This is one approach – that conflicting traditions serve to sharpen our understanding and help us arrive at the truth.

However, could it not just be that what has actually been passed down to us represents a variety of opinions? Is it not the case that the preservation of these conflicting traditions actually serves to demonstrate the authenticity of multiple Jewish traditions regarding these philosophical or theological issues?

COUNTER-TEXT
Conflicting Texts Cannot Be Resolved
Anyone who studies our Talmud knows that regarding the disagreements among the commentators there are no absolute proofs, and generally there are no irrefutable objections. For this branch of wisdom does not allow for clear demonstrations as does mathematics.[2]

According to Ramban, human reason does not always lend itself to resolving these matters in a way that can be proven to be true. Commentators debating these issues could only express the views about which they were passionate, but generally could not prove one way or another that their understanding was *the* truth in the matter.

One More Story; One More Talmudic Parallel

The I-35w Mississippi River bridge was an eight-lane, 1,907-foot bridge which carried Interstate 35w across the Mississippi River in Minneapolis, Minnesota. Completed in 1967, the bridge was Minnesota's fifth-busiest, carrying 140,000 vehicles daily. At 6:05 p.m. on August 1, 2007, during the evening rush hour, the bridge suddenly collapsed, falling into the river and onto its banks. Thirteen people died and approximately one hundred more were injured.

What a strange calamity. A modern, seemingly well-engineered bridge in a major metropolitan area collapsed in a moment without any forewarning of danger.

Of course, despite the fact that something similar could happen to any of us at any time, people began to wonder about the possible message. Was it God's will?

---

2. Ramban, Introduction to his *Milchamot Hashem*.

The Westboro Baptist Church of Topeka, Kansas, staged protests at funerals of victims of the bridge collapse to affirm that God made the bridge fall because he hates America, and especially Minnesota, because of its tolerance of homosexuality. Shirley Phelps Roper, the pastor's daughter and one of the attorneys for the church, said that America, and Minnesota especially, had alienated God through their tolerance for homosexuality, and that the bridge collapse was an act of God's vengeance. In her words:

> The bridge stood in place by the word of God and it fell by the word of God.... Each of these little events is just a harbinger of the coming destruction of this American experiment. We are delivering the final call of the doomed nation.[3]

It seems to me that the following Talmudic disagreement is one more excellent example of how varied traditions existed among the rabbis as to how we are to relate to God's role in traumatic events like the I-35 bridge collapse.

TEXT
Crossing Over the Bridge
When are human beings examined?

Said Reish Lakish: "When they cross over a bridge."

A bridge and nothing else?

Rather, better to say, anytime they face something that is similar to crossing a bridge.

Rav would not cross a bridge where a heathen was sitting. He said, "Lest judgment be visited upon the heathen, and I be seized together with him."

Shmuel would cross a bridge *only* when a heathen was upon it, saying, "Satan has no power over two nations [simultaneously]."

Rabbi Yannai examined [the bridge] and then crossed over.[4]

Each of these rabbinic scholars of the third/fourth century offered a different prescription for safely crossing a bridge. However, their difference

---

3. "Fred Phelps Is Coming," *Twin Cities Daily Planet*, August 7, 2007; http://www.tcdailyplanet.net/article/2007/08/07/fred-phelps-coming.html.
4. Babylonian Talmud, Shabbat 32a.

of opinion was not about safety. Each of their positions offers a different take on God's role in tragedy.

To begin, Reish Lakish sets the tone. He indicates that during the moments in our lives when we are more susceptible to danger, that is when God will choose to mete out deserved punishment. In other words, God takes advantage of such circumstances to address His own agendas with us.

This complicates matters. A person who falls from a dangerous height, or gets hurt while engaging in a dangerous activity, might want to blame his misfortune on the activity or the circumstances surrounding it. However, Reish Lakish teaches that such misfortune could certainly be an act of God, and one should seriously take into consideration the possibility that an accident and the suffering that ensues are meant as divine punishment or rebuke.

According to Reish Lakish, every misfortune can be interpreted to be the hand of God in our lives. We cannot know for sure.

Rav adds another dimension to the tragic bridge scenario. He suggests that not only might a person be judged and punished in the context of such dangerous circumstances, but "heathen," gentile sinners may be targeted for punishment under such circumstances without regard for someone who is not at all deserving of punishment, someone who just happens to be there on the bridge at the same time. Such an innocent person could be caught up in a punishment not specifically directed his way.

This position implies that one must consider that death or suffering is not always the direct result of the victim's guilt. In such a case, God does not purposefully take the life of the victim. He does not intend to punish all who suffer. Innocent people can become the unfortunate victims of the collateral damage of another's punishment, simply because they find themselves in the wrong place at the wrong time.

According to Rav, not every misfortune should be interpreted to be the hand of God in our personal lives. Some people suffer – even die – as a result of such misfortune. In the end, we cannot know for sure.

Shmuel offers an interesting twist on this same scenario that also tests the limits of our beliefs. Here it is suggested that one who might very well be slated for suffering or even death would do well to take advantage of a loophole in the system. Since Satan, the adversarial angel, has no power over two nationalities at the same time, by crossing the bridge or engaging in some other potentially dangerous activity with a member of another nationality, one can essentially outwit Satan and circumvent one's fate.

According to Shmuel, we human beings have the ability to manipulate our own destiny according to the circumstances of a given situation. There are precautions we can take which can, essentially, steer our fate in a favorable direction. Knowing the rules of the game, we can outmaneuver even God's adversarial angel.

Finally, this brings us to Rabbi Yannai's teaching. According to Rabbi Yannai, accidents represent neither the hand of God directed at the victim, nor the result of collateral damage from a punishment directed at others. Rather, accidents are just that – accidents, the result of poor planning, poor preparation, or poor decisions. Rabbi Yannai refuses to read more into it than that.

According to Rabbi Yannai, the way to avoid unfortunate tragedy is to be careful. That is not to say that we can always take the necessary precautions. There are dangerous activities that we engage in all the time, permitted to do so by the Talmudic principle of *keivan shedashin bo rabim*,[5] which states that even though an activity is inherently risky, since society in general deems the risk to be reasonable, it is thus halachically permissible to take such a risk. Crossing a highway bridge would be an example of such an acceptable risk. Human error and miscalculations are an inextricable part of the conditions of human existence.

Given this reality, Rabbi Yannai maintains that it is our responsibility to take whatever precautions are necessary, and to refrain from relying on miracles. When an accident occurs, it need not be interpreted as anything more than an accident, an unfortunate by-product of our human condition.

There Is No Right Understanding

So what do you think? Who was right?

There are those who would like to say that there is no one truth, that everything is true. As a rule, Judaism absolutely rejects this position. Judaism has presented the world with a Torah and a system of living that emanates from God, the source of all truth – *His Torah is truth and His prophets spoke truth*.

There are, however, certain areas in which the question of who is "right" really is not relevant. In these specific areas, we find significant tolerance

---

5.   Babylonian Talmud, Yevamot 72a. This principle is discussed at length in chapter 3.

for multiple opinions. No particular position is more right than any other, and most importantly, there is no need to make such a determination.

I once again cite the words of Rambam, who seems to have dealt with such differences and contradictions in the following way:

> In every disagreement between sages, where there are no practical ramifications, rather it is only a matter of belief, then there is no need to decide according to one of them [over the other].[6]

When our tradition presents us with multiple approaches to issues like the ones we have been addressing in this book, Rambam emphasized that there is *no need to decide according to one of them over the other.* Together they present us with a continuum of beliefs, all of them well founded within authentic Jewish theology.

Speaking of Rambam, there were certain rabbinic scholars who were highly critical of Rambam's thoughts and philosophical approaches. For instance, a twentieth-century scholar and writer named Rabbi Zeev Yavetz wrote a scathing criticism of Rambam's *Guide for the Perplexed*, claiming that his writings were outside of what could be accepted as authentic Jewish ideas. In response to this attack, Rabbi Abraham Isaac HaKohen Kook, the first Ashkenazi chief rabbi of the British Mandate for Palestine, wrote that Yavetz was out of line.

> Decision in this arena is left up to the temperament and the spiritual perspectives of each and every one, according to his nature as a human being. There is no doubt that there are some people for whom certain ideas resonate well, connecting their hearts to holiness and purity, to faith and service, to Torah and its commandments, while there are others for whom particular other ideas serve to bring their hearts close to all of these holy and lofty notions. And given that the ideas elucidated in the *Guide* are in line with a spirit of holiness, strength of faith and holy devotion to divine service…then there is no wonder that there are a great many among Israel for whom these ideas will resonate. And if there are others, who in good faith are unable to relate their system of values to all of the ideas articulated in the *Guide*, then they have the right to align their thoughts with great scholars of Israel who have paved a different path; however, God

---

6. Rambam, *Commentary on the Mishnah*, Sanhedrin 10:3.

forbid that we should speak negatively...about these ideas, that were sanctified by the spirit of Rambam, of blessed memory.[7]

Rabbi Kook understood that in the realm of the philosophical, Judaism makes room for multiple approaches. Individuals will gravitate to different options, and in this way a maximum number of people will finds themselves maintaining a strong Jewish identity and a hardy faith in God. In fact, it is the presence of these multiple voices within Jewish tradition that has preserved its magnificent versatility and relevance.

Rabbi Yechiel Michel Epstein (1829–1907), author of the *Aruch HaShulchan*, put it this way:

> On the contrary, this is the glory of our pure and holy Torah. The entire Torah is called a song, and the splendor of a song is when there are different voices; this is the essence of harmony. Anyone who sails the sea of the Talmud will discern the harmony rising from all the different voices.[8]

When you honestly consider the whole issue of suffering, you realize that there can be no other way.

No two people experience suffering in exactly the same way. Each person is different, each of us is the product of a unique set of personal circumstances, and so it is no wonder that our rabbis came to different conclusions as to the source, the purpose, and the way we are to deal with suffering in our world. We find such a position in the words of the Vilna Gaon:

> Each and every person has his own unique path to follow. For people differ one from the other in their intellect, as well as in their faces, and the nature of two people is not the same. During the time of the prophets, people would go to the prophets to inquire of God. The prophet would tell each person, based upon prophecy, the path that he should follow according to the root of his soul and the nature of his body. And when prophecy ceased, the *ruach hakodesh* [holy spirit] rested upon Israel; each person is told by his own counsel how to conduct himself, for *ruach hakodesh* is found in every person.[9]

---

7. Abraham Isaac HaKohen Kook, "L'achduto shel HaRambam," in *Maamarei HaRaayah* (Jerusalem: Golda Katz Foundation, 1984), 1:108.

8. Introduction to *Aruch HaShulchan*, Choshen Mishpat.

9. Vilna Gaon, commentary on Proverbs 16:4.

In other words, it is our calling to consult our own inner counsel, to reflect on what happens in our own lives and the lives of those with whom we have shared this planet. It is helpful to consider what others have thought; it is important to consult the teachings of our tradition, to hear the voices of our great rabbinic scholars as they wrestled with the challenges of good and evil, looked to God for salvation, and asked the inevitable question: *God, where is my miracle?*

However, it seems that none of us are expected to adopt one position over another. That is to say, Jewish tradition has preserved a variety of approaches in a concerted effort to give each individual the privilege of finding an answer that suits his or her own inner convictions.

Two God-fearing people can both live through the very same traumatic incident, can suffer the same loss, can endure the torturous pains of the very same disease, and yet look upon their suffering from very different perspectives – one sees it as a punishment from God, the other, as the result of the human condition.

Neither is more righteous than the other. Neither has greater faith in God than the other. Both can find their place within the ancient traditions of our people.

I have not come to write this book in order to say everyone is "right." I don't see how that is possible. I realize that although all of these positions have their place within our tradition, in any given situation, only one is actually correct. That is to say, either God is punishing the sufferer, or He is not. Either the accident is part of God's divine plan, a plan beyond our comprehension, or it is not. Either the suffering is for the purpose of leading the sufferer to engage in self-judgment, or it is not.

I agree that we can't explain what has happened by applying all perspectives at the same time – they are often in conflict. Rather, my point is that because we can never know for sure what, if anything, is the purpose of suffering or tragedy, we are on our own to consider the situation and to relate to the events in the way that makes the most sense to us.

Personally, I live my life like this:

When something *good* happens, I certainly know that God could be the source of this goodness (even if I do not know for sure). I thank God for His kindness and for the many good things with which I have been blessed. I feel even better, relating this kindness to God's love for me.

On the other hand, when something *bad* happens, I cannot say for sure that it is from God. My preference, in most cases, is to assume that it is not – that it is not in line with what God in His great love for me would want to happen. Therefore, I do not blame God, and instead, turn to Him for support and strength as I face the challenge before me.

I like to believe that in this way I maximize sanctification of God's name – giving Him credit for the good, and holding Him blameless for the bad.

Again, what will speak to and inspire one individual may very well raise the ire of another. I have seen it happen time and time again. And even if one approach is ultimately right and one is ultimately wrong, in issues of faith, there is no need to judge.

Rabbi Chaim Navon, a contemporary Israeli scholar, may have said it best:

> If we recognize the importance of individual accomplishment and autonomous personal development in the worship of God, then it may sometimes be preferable for a person to adopt ideas that are clearly mistaken, but which he arrived at on his own, rather than blindly accept true ideas that he heard from others. When a person develops as an individual and in an independent manner, the intensity of his service of God will be greater.[10]

Applying this idea to your own quest for understanding in the face of suffering, it is my belief that you must personally engage the complexities of this dilemma and come to your own conclusions, develop your own personal framework for dealing with the inexplicable tragedies that come your way, and do so in a way that reinforces your faith in God.

This book has been an effort to present the varying and conflicting approaches of our scholars throughout the generations, as well as my own personal thinking and interpretations of this timeless quandary. Even if some readers will challenge me, accusing me at times of being "clearly mistaken," to this point I can wholeheartedly testify: this inquiry and all that it has taught me has only served to heighten the intensity of my faith and to deepen my own personal service of God.

---

10. Rabbi Chaim Navon, "Lecture #13: Controversy," Yeshivat Har Etzion Virtual Beit Midrash; http://vbm-torah.org/archive/philhalak/13mhal.rtf.

Even though I walk through the valley
of the shadow of death,
I fear no evil, for You are with me;
Your rod and Your staff, they comfort me.

You prepare a table before me
in the presence of my enemies;
You have anointed my head with oil;
My cup overflows.

Surely goodness and loving-kindness
will follow me all the days of my life,
And I will dwell in the house of the Lord forever.

(Psalms 23:4–6)